Published by
Cazu Productions and Publishing
mail@alcazu.com

ISBN-13: 978-1523885237
ISBN-10: 1523885238

Challenge

These images derive from a circumnavigation
of the Cornish Coastline. Collectively they
form a puzzle. The riddle that resides within
this collection of pictures and is also clued
within the written words is solvable. It is
nothing more than a three worded answer.
If you can solve this riddle e-mail:
mail@alcazu.com with your solution.
The first to be the correct will be rewarded
with an original artwork, the following ten
correct solutions with be rewarded with a
high quality print signed by the artist.
Good luck.

Background image
Electric Sky
Watercolour 340 x 540 mm

The Riddle

What is the best way to know exactly where
you are and how to map accurately to where
you want to go to?

Wave Scribble *Pencil 250 x 250 mm*

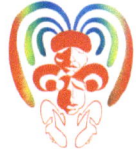

Daybreak *Watercolour 340 x 540 mm*

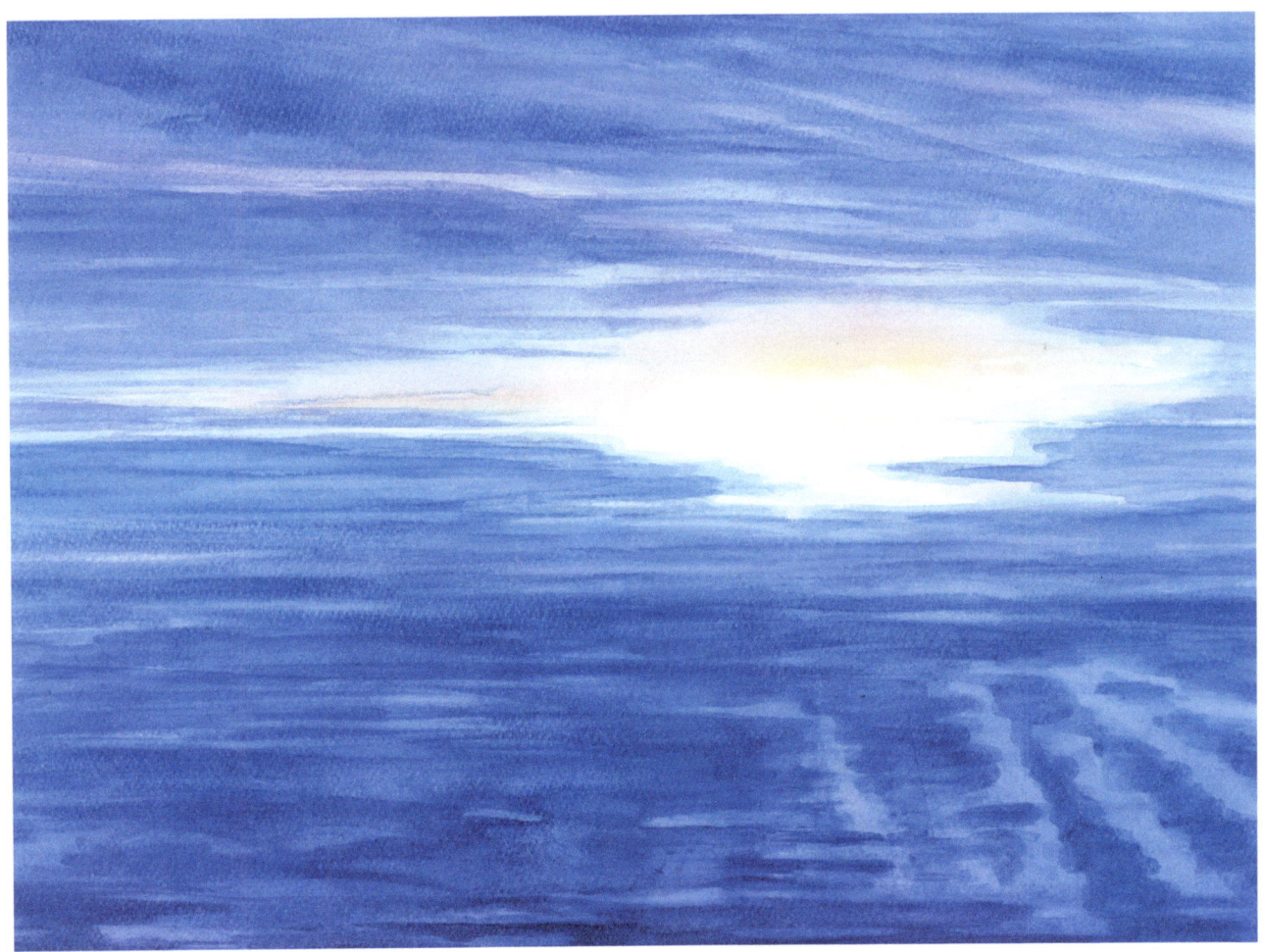

Every new day begins with a single speck of light on the horizon. Just like the seed of a new hope or dream, it soon expands and starts to flow. Before very long it fills the sky.

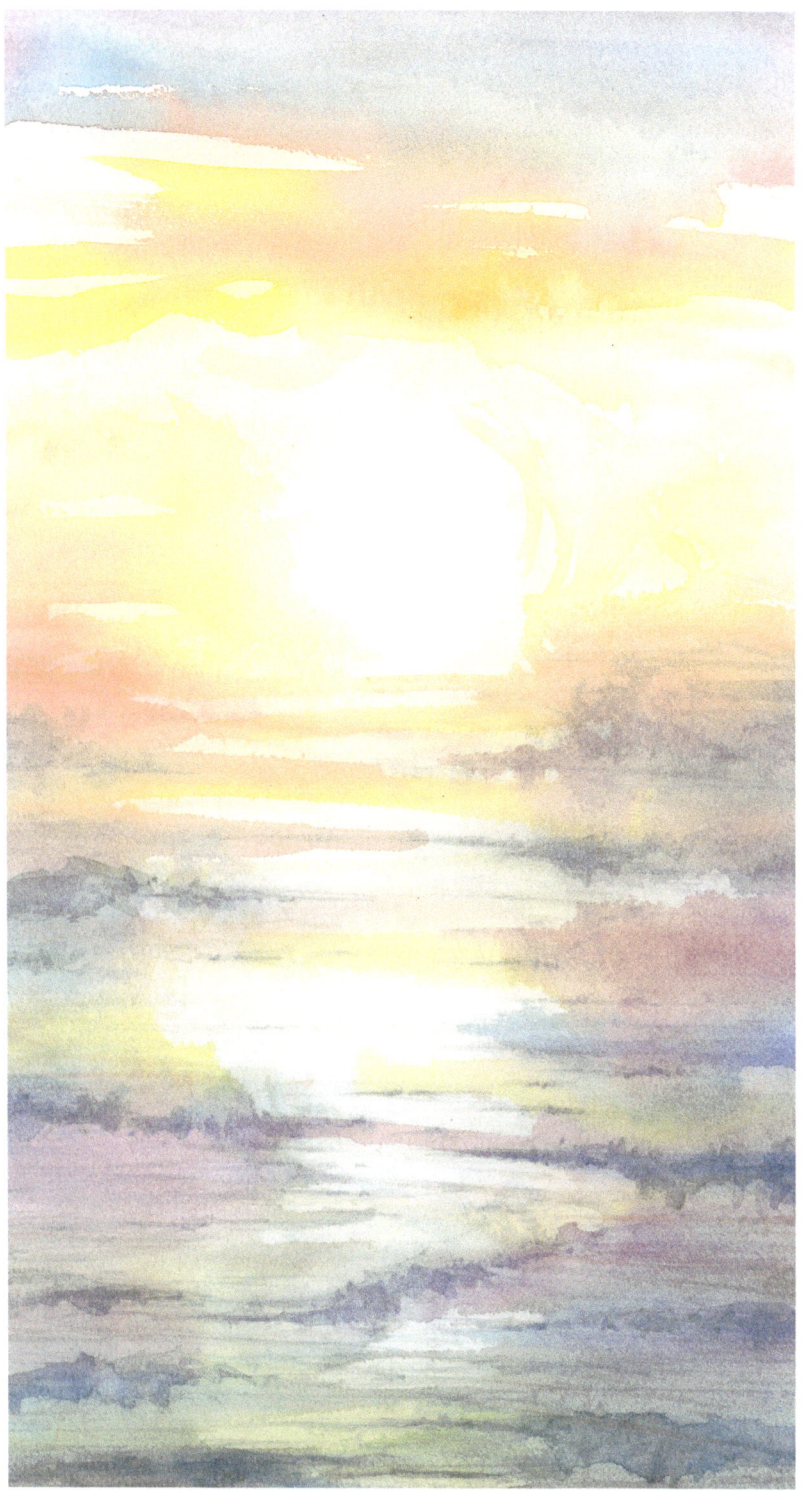

Morning Joy
Watercolour 540 x 340 mm

Bringing light and warmth the sun rises above the ocean and embarks on it's daily passage across the sky. On this day it invites me to set foot upon my own intended journey around the Cornish Coast.

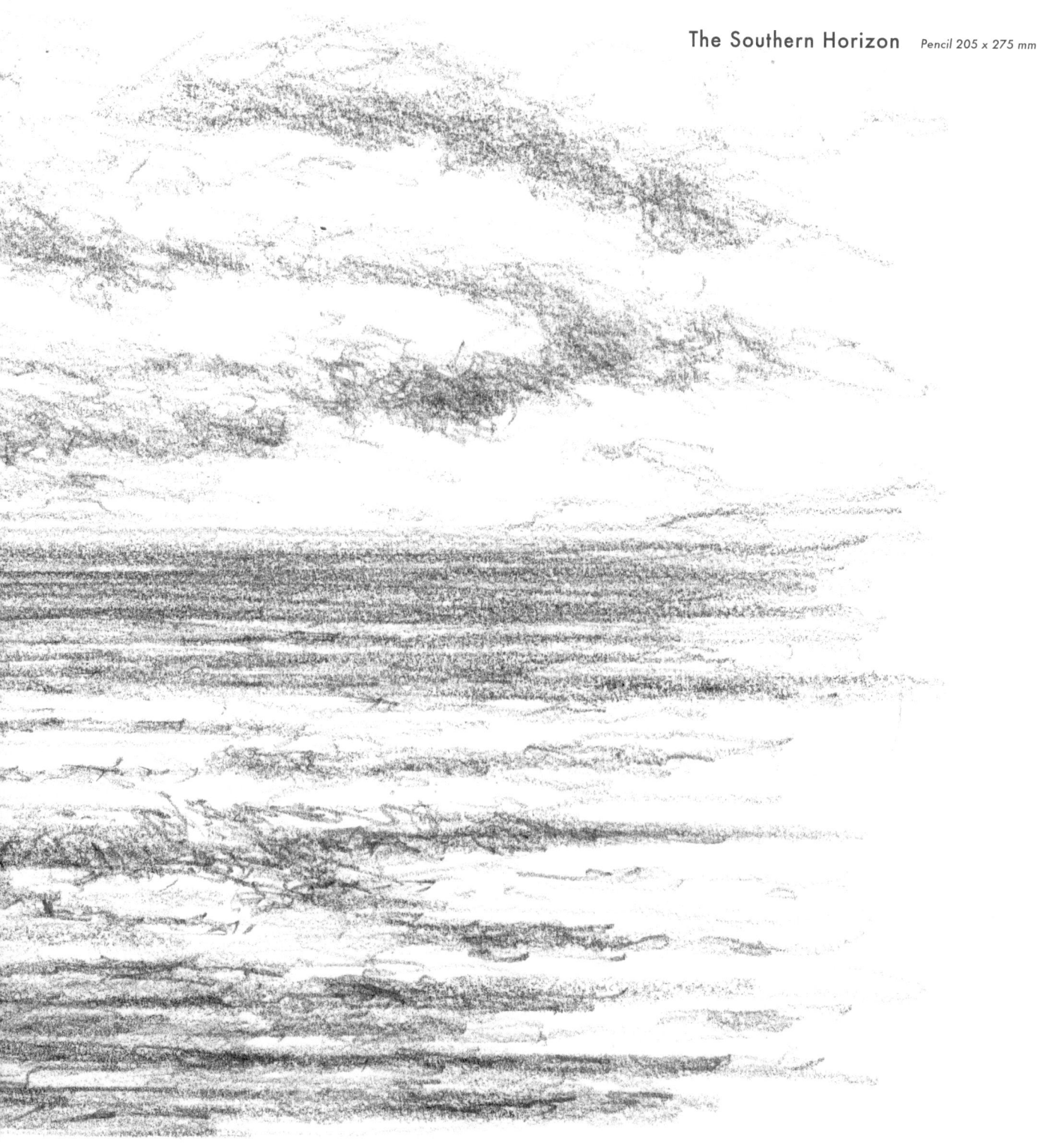

The Southern Horizon   *Pencil 205 x 275 mm*

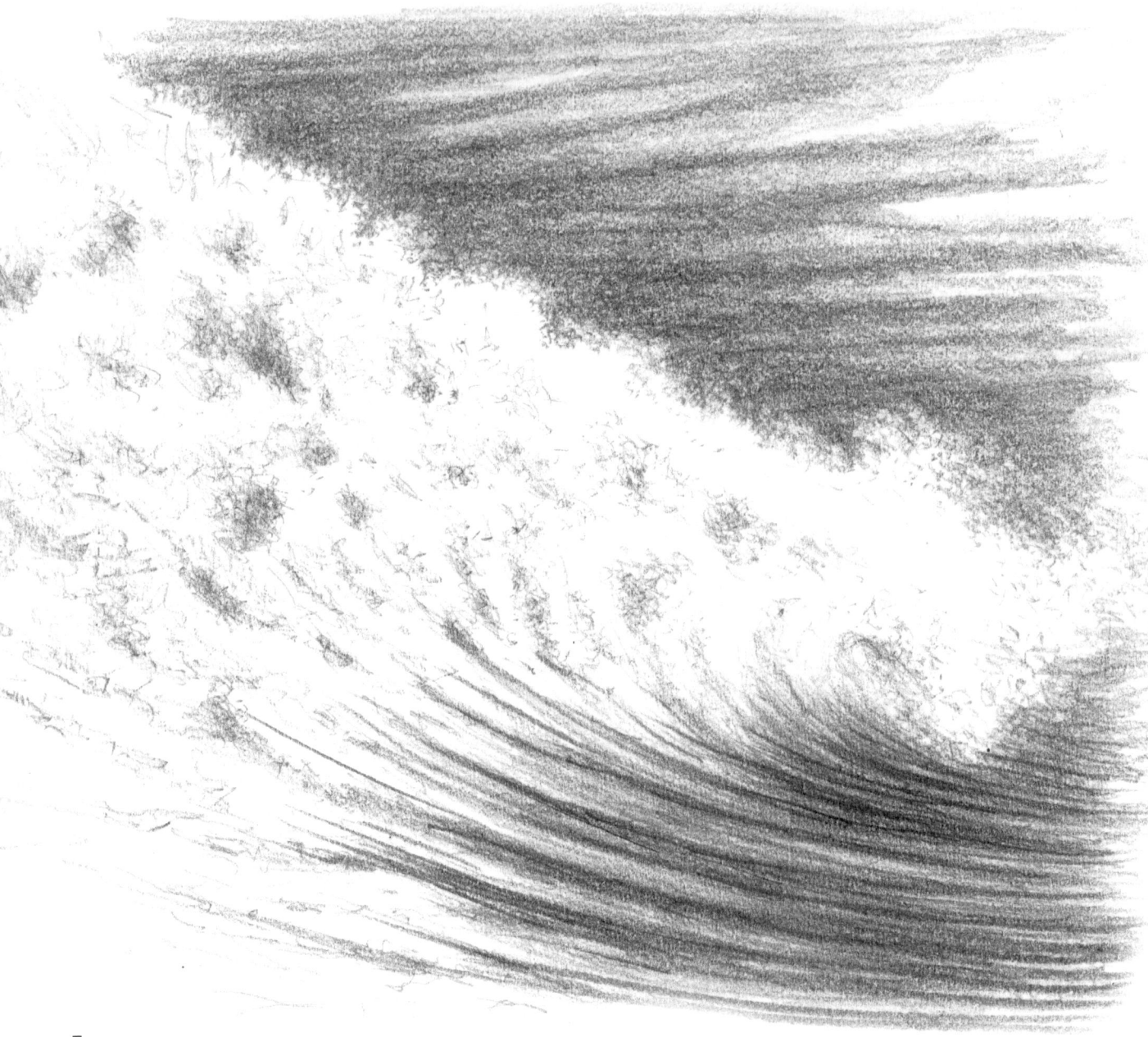

Energy Pencil 205 x 275 mm

Polperro *Watercolour 340 x 540 mm*

I began my journey from the sheltered southern shoreline far to the east and near to Polperro. I swam in the calm waters that are overlooked by the tall craggy rocks, after which I rendered my first painting of this adventure and series of pictures.

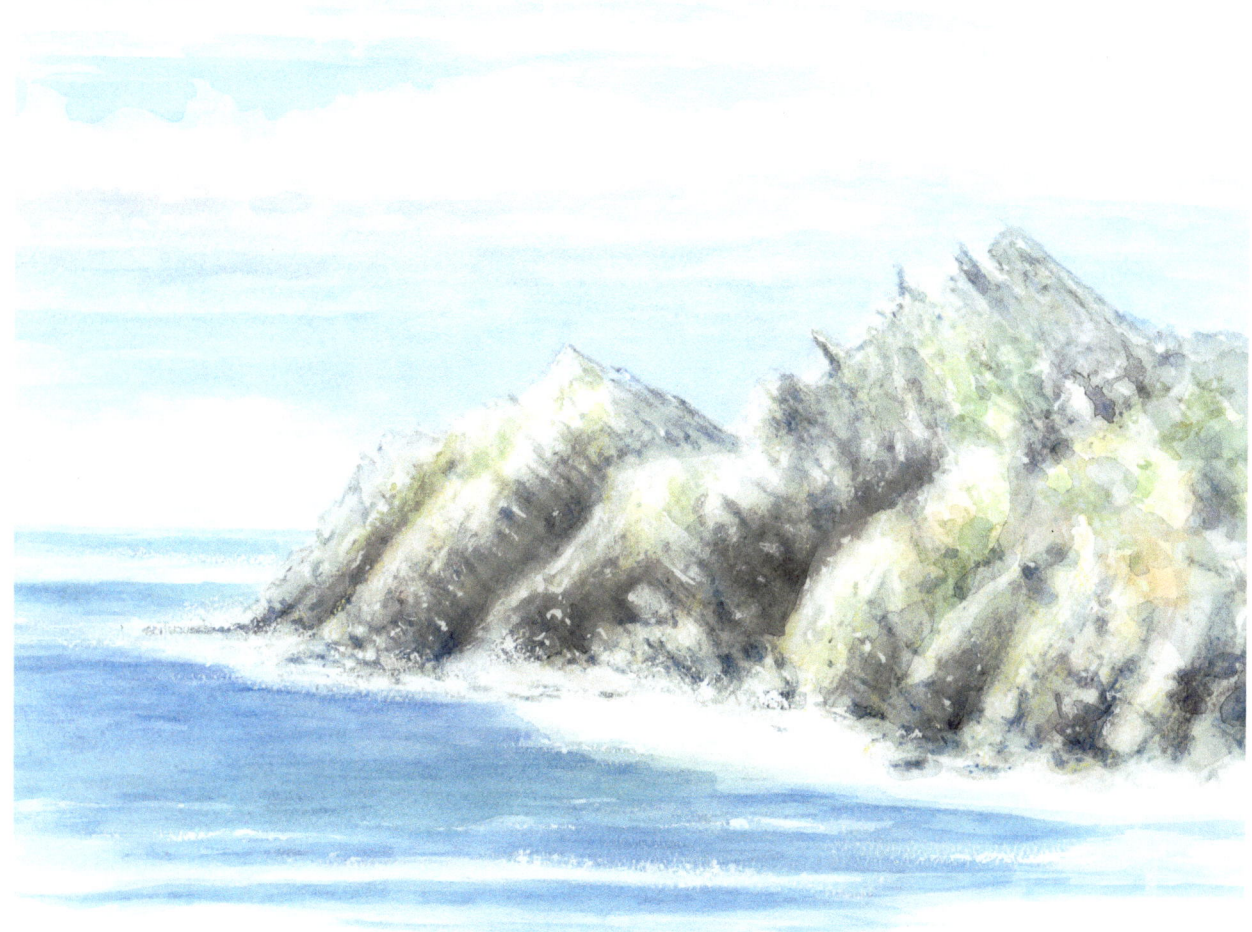

To investigate these rock formations must be a geologist's dream. They were formed millions of years ago and have been sculpted by weather and sea ever since. At Polperro they rise from the ocean with a majestic presence. At the hand of nature what a beautiful place this planet of ours has become.

Red Strokes Watercolour 340 x 540 mm

Sometimes the ocean seems to drink up the colours of the setting sun and deliver them to the shoreline. The ever changing yellows, reds, and, purples seem to be captured within the waves until they break and add white to nature's colour pallet. Before long the sun disappears below the horizon and the red strokes end until another day and time.

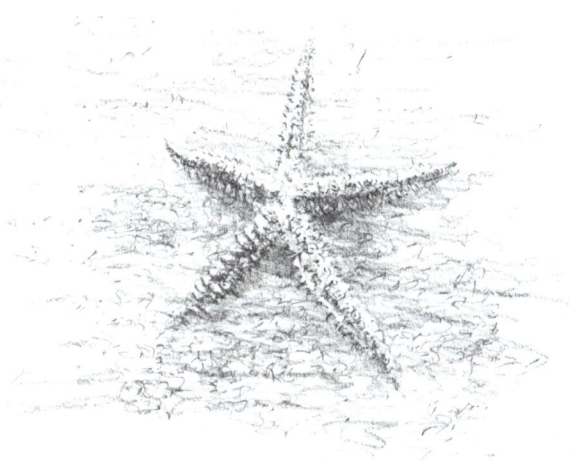

Starfish Pencil 205 x 205 mm

The retreating tide often leaves behind marine life. The rock pools accommodate these small fascinating creatures until the tide returns.

Saddle Rocks *Watercolour 340 x 540 mm*

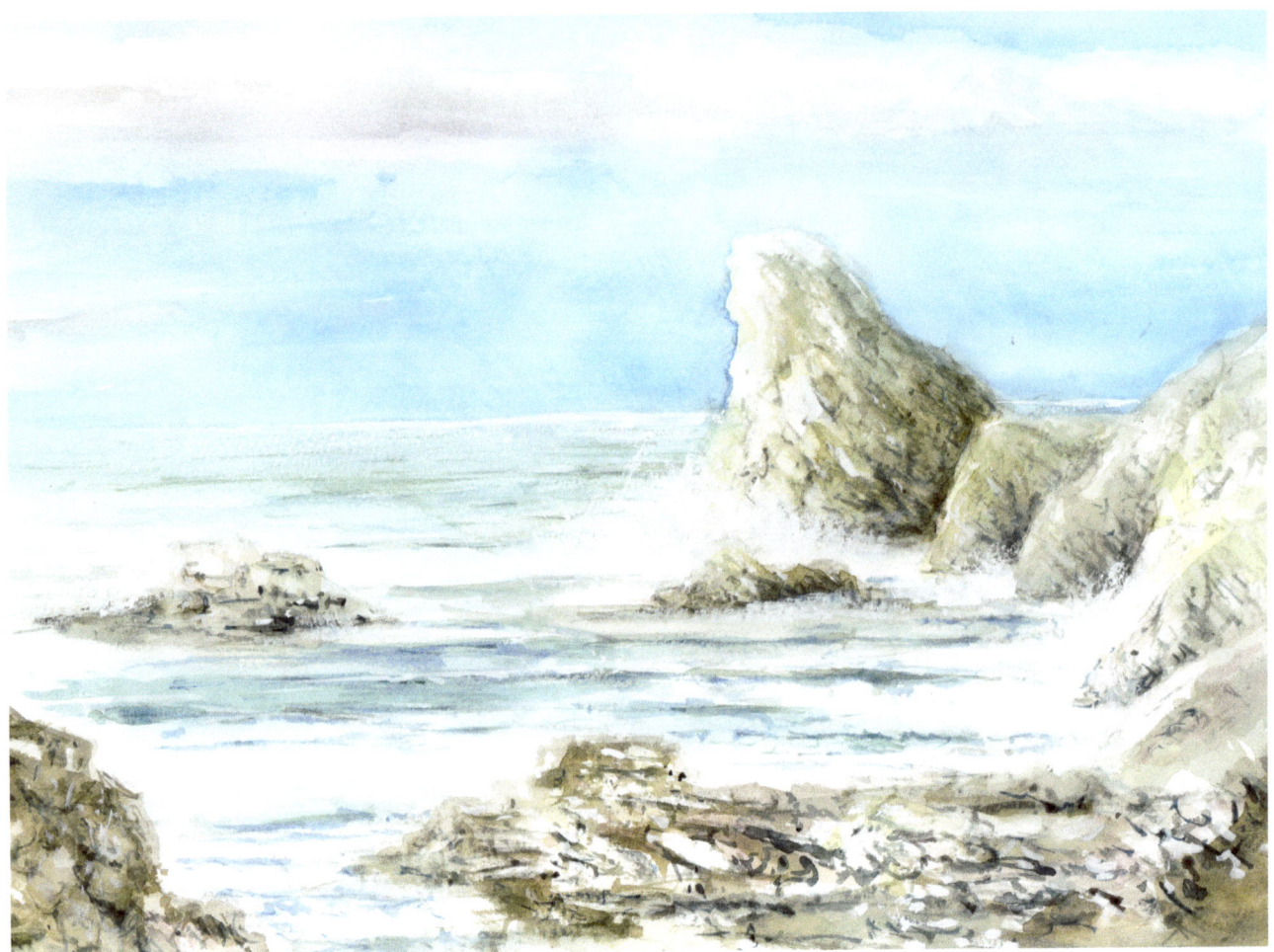

From Polperro I travelled north across land and arrived on the wild wind swept north shore of Cornwall. My destination was Saddle Rocks at Tintagel. Again I swam but the waves were high and sported white tops as far out to sea as the eye could see. The channel between the rocks was not navigable for swimming on that day so I soon retreated from the ocean and painted my second picture.

Light Through The Canopy, Tintagel

Pencil 275 x 205 mm

If the legends are to be believed Tintagel is where King Arthur presided over his honourable and loyal knights of the Round Table. I would like to think that Queen Guinevere once stood upon this spot and gazed out on this dramatic dance of the ocean.

Saint Agnus *Watercolour 340 x 540 mm*

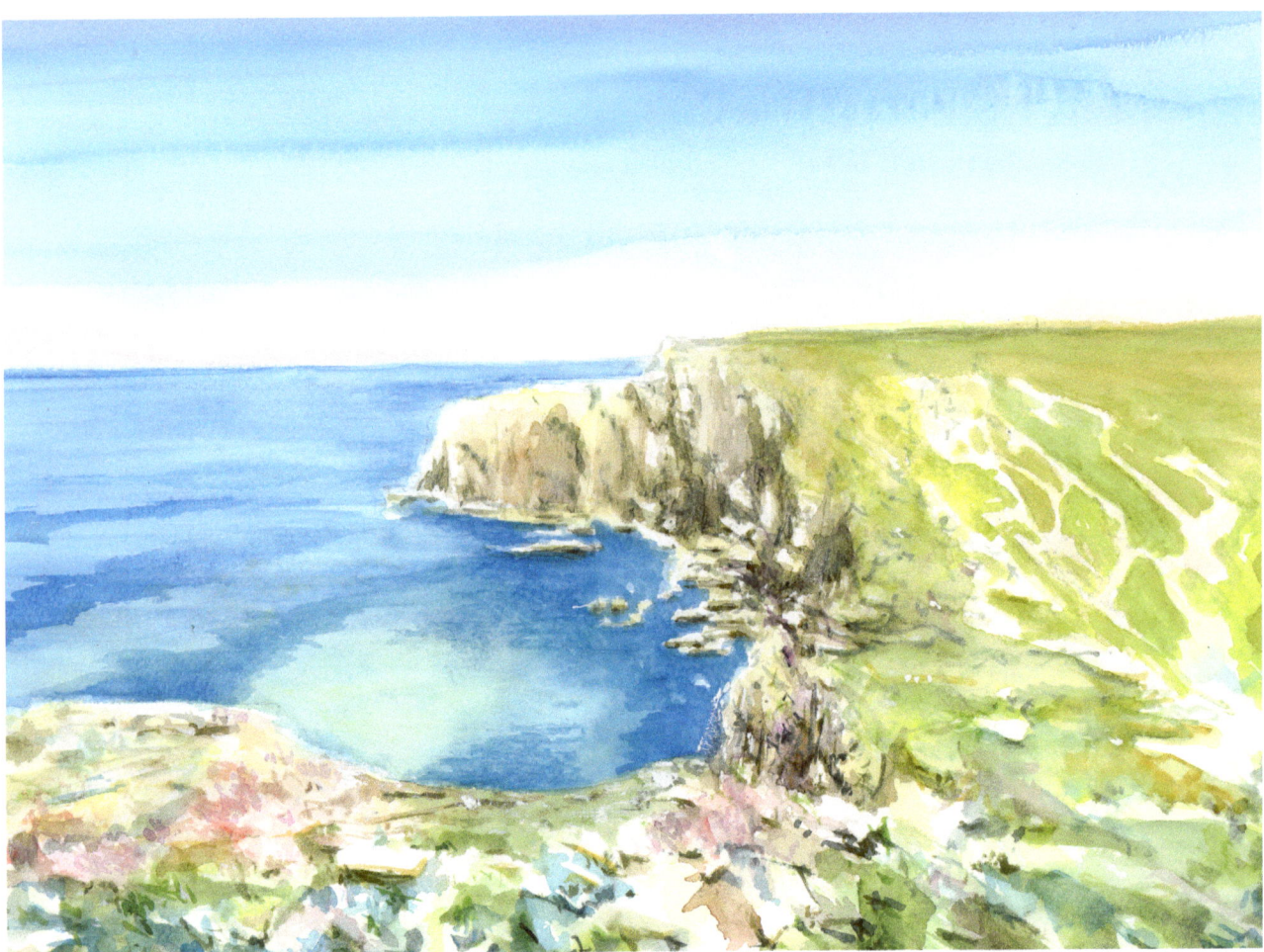

The following morning I headed west and onto Saint Agnus, a place I know well and love. From the high coastal path I painted the view to the east and around the magnificent headland. Pulled out my guitar and improvised, attempting to synchronize the sounds that I made with the natural noises of the sea and wind.

Reflection *Pencil 205 x 275 mm*

The first evidence of human inhabitants in this area dates back more than seven thousand years. This is in the form of hand tools made from flint. There are also relics here that exist from the bronze and iron ages. The area is also famed from it's history of tin mining, not to mention it's outstanding beauty.

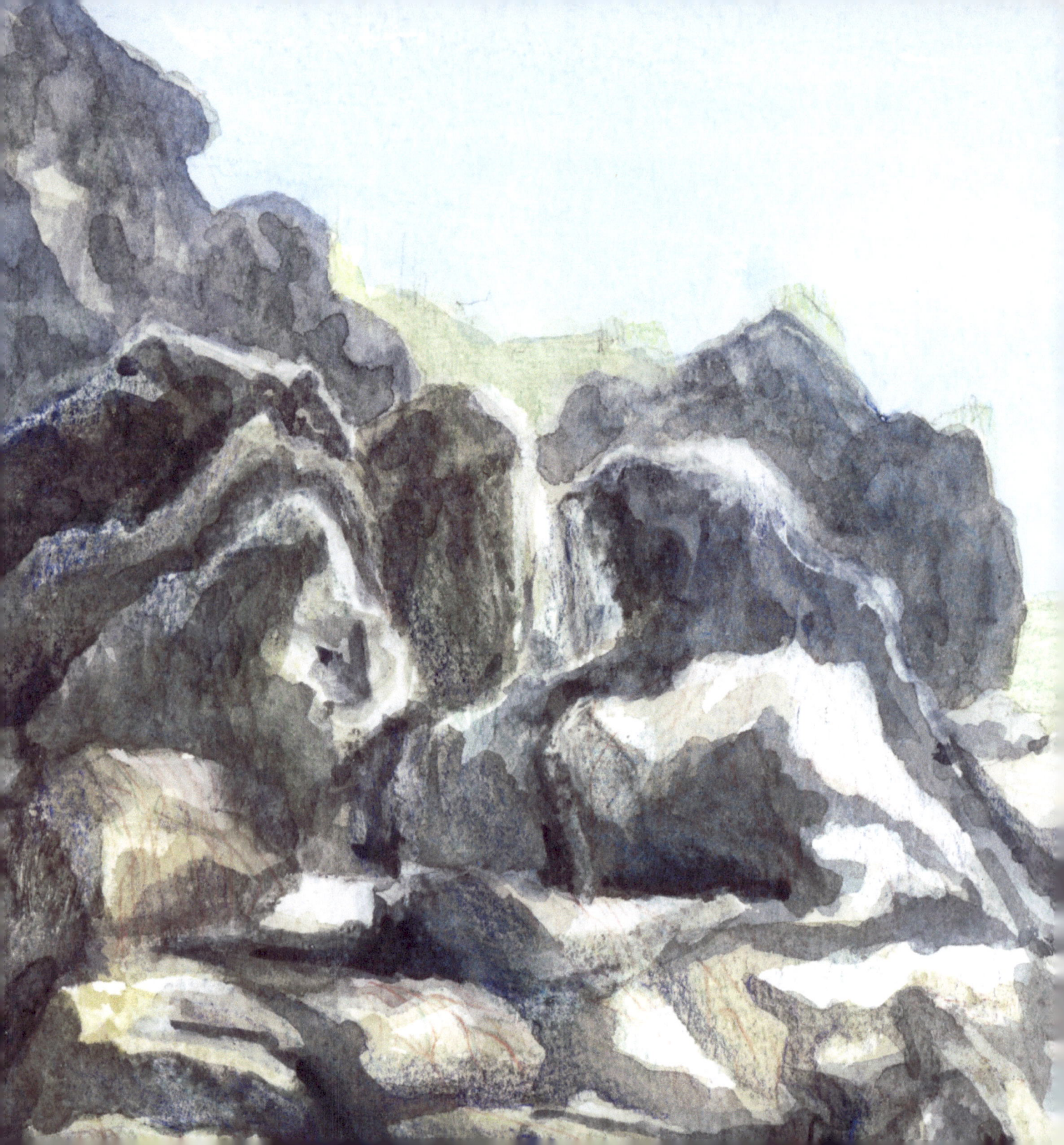

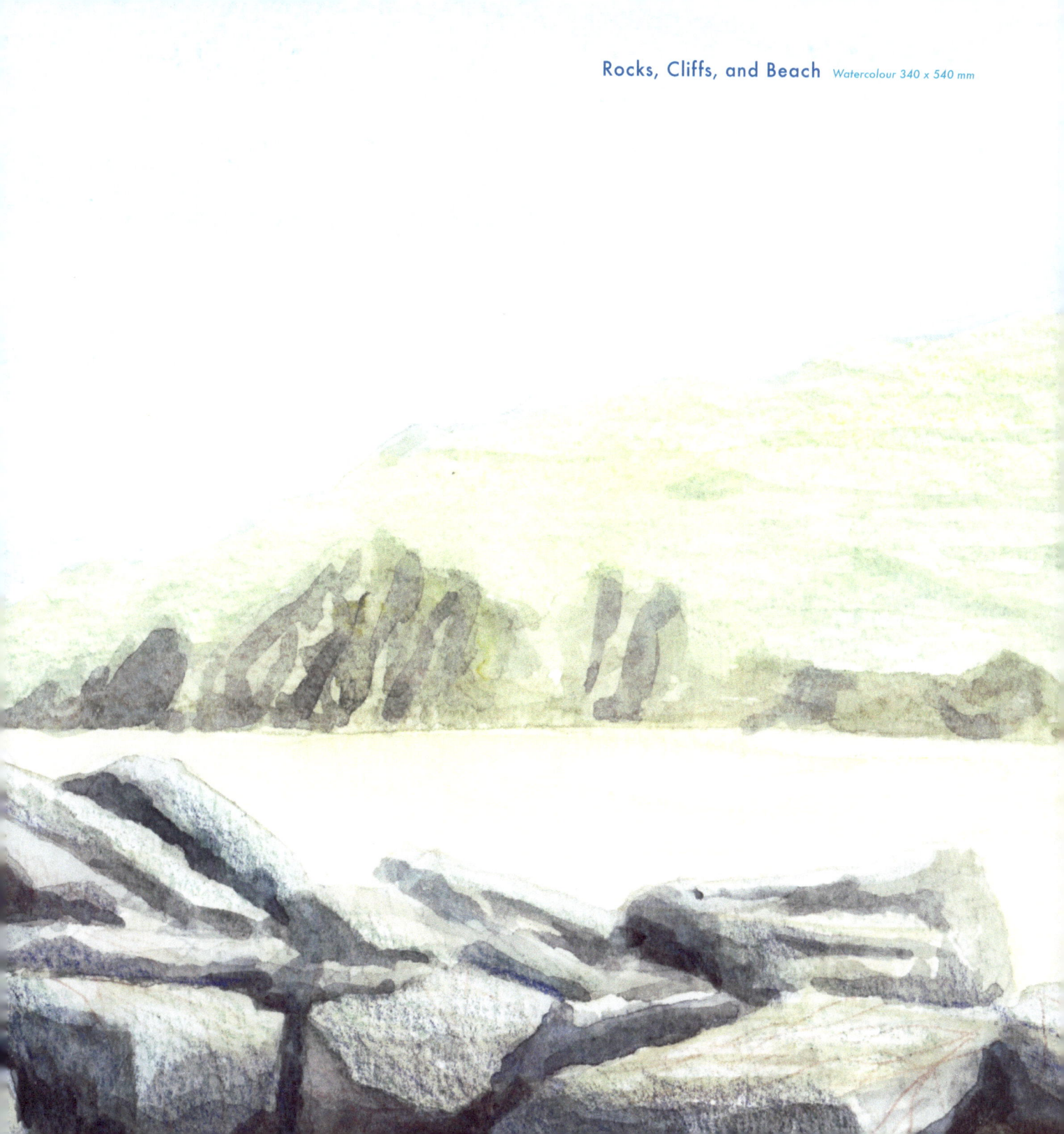

Viewing The Terrain

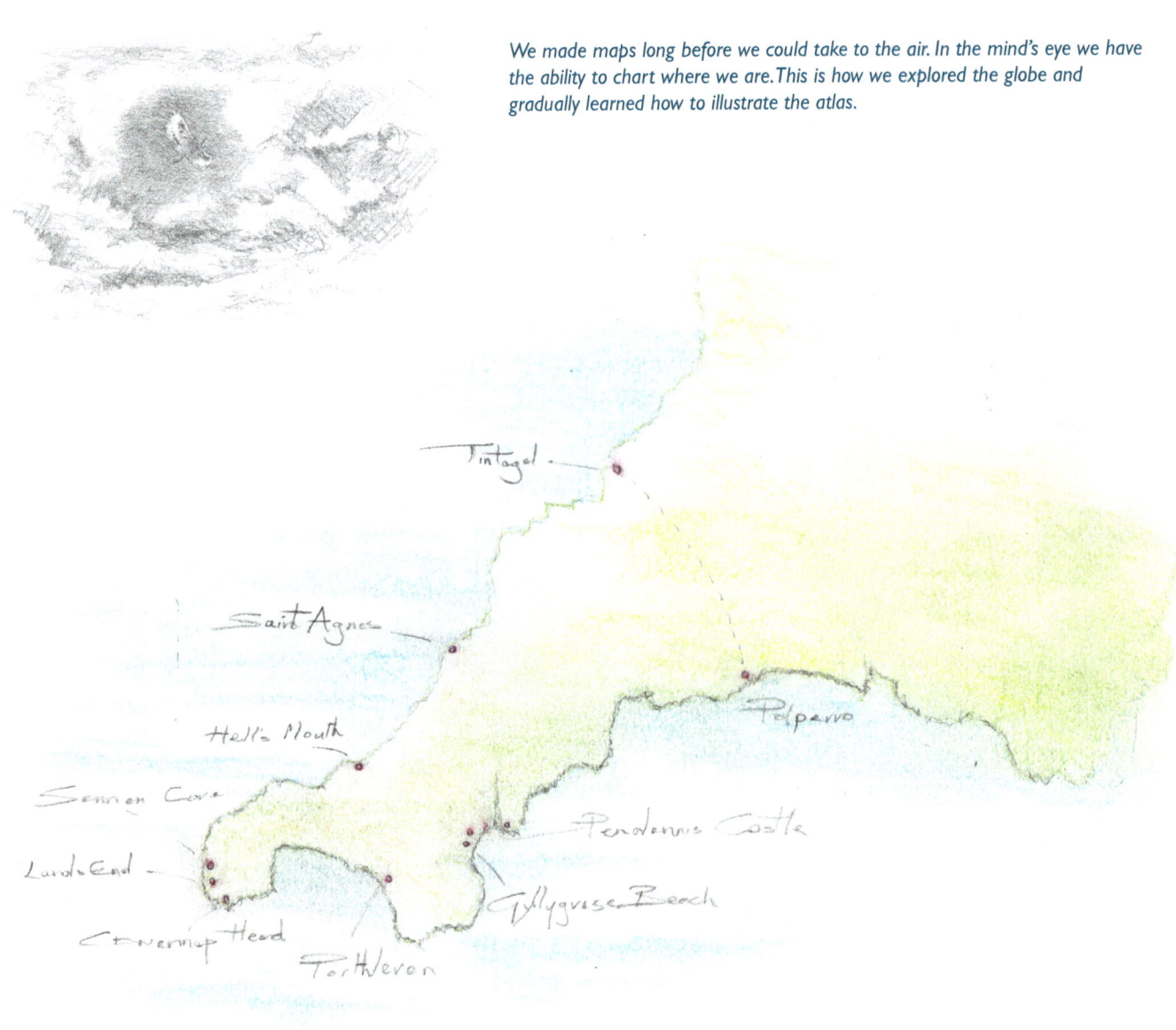

We made maps long before we could take to the air. In the mind's eye we have the ability to chart where we are. This is how we explored the globe and gradually learned how to illustrate the atlas.

Tintagel

Saint Agnes

Polperro

Hell's Mouth

Sennen Cove

Pendennis Castle

Land's End

Gyllyngvase Beach

Gwennap Head

Porthleven

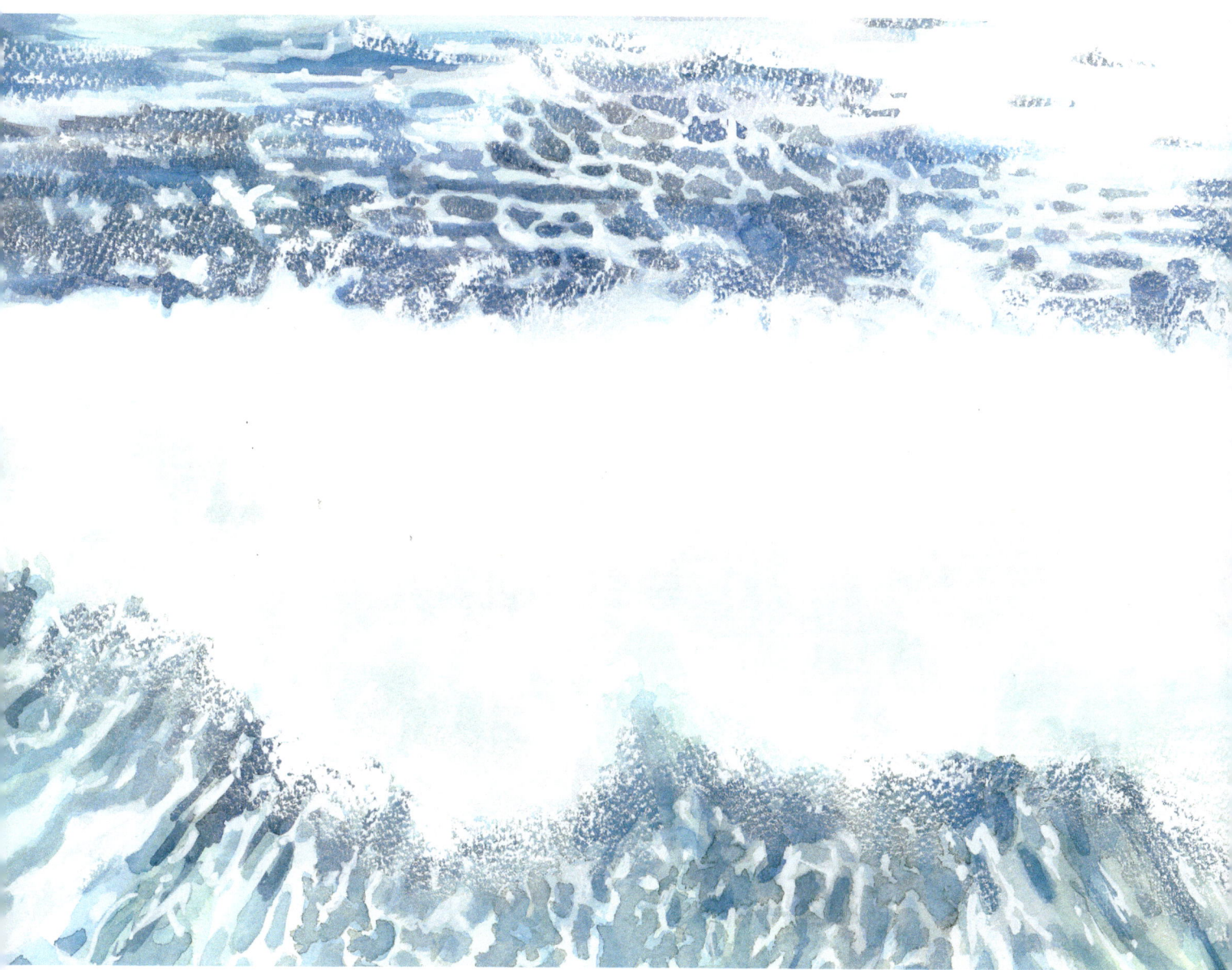

Incoming Tide *Watercolour 340 x 540 mm*

The Cornish Peninsula, surrounded by water has always isolated this corner of England. It has protected the county from much, it has made the inhabitants very dependent on the sea, and it's history is rich indeed. I personally want to live nowhere else.

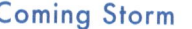

Coming Storm 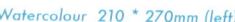 *Watercolour 210 * 270mm (left)*

Way finding inland is not as easy as merely following the coastline. On the high hills that rise from the seashore the weather can change for the worse very quickly. The westerly wind is often kind but can at times bring unbridled storms that have built heavily as they crossed the vast Atlantic Ocean.

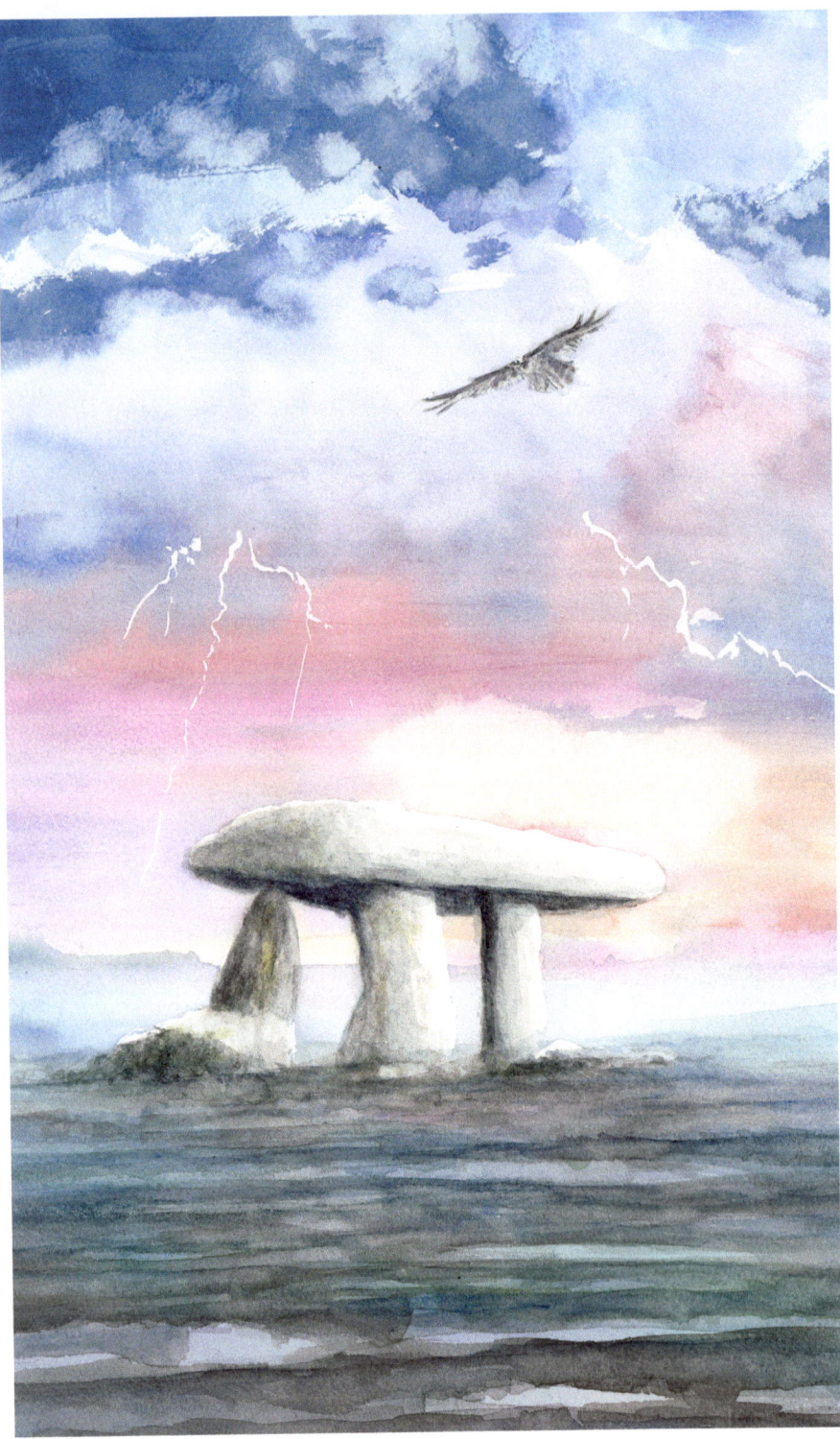

Lanyon Quoit
Watercolour 540 x 340 mm

Thousands of years ago standing stones were erected by our ancestors, Cornwall boasts many of these petrified structures. It is commonly believed that Lanyon Quoit is an historical burial tomb.

Hell's Mouth *Watercolour 340 x 540 mm*

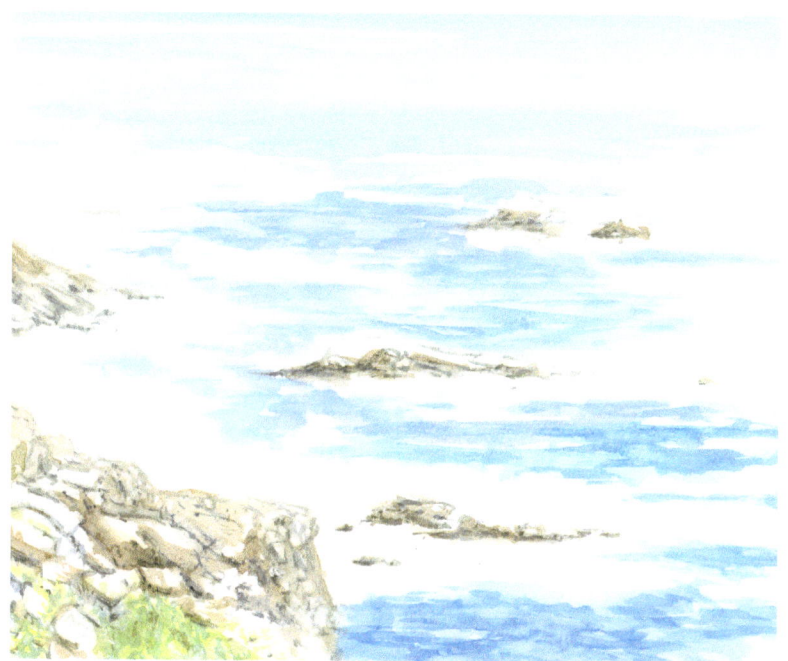

The next day I ventured down along the coast to Hell's Mouth. There was where I made my first climb of the trip. I had acquired a rigger's harness from Falmouth Docks, this made it possible for me to carry on my back my guitar and painting equipment. From the top of the cliff face I painted the waters below me as they crashed upon the rocks that protruded from the white foam offshore. I also wrote a tune that I shall name 'Hell's Mouth'.

No prizes for guessing how this place got it's name. The Cornish coast is notorious for it's reputation among seafarers. It is littered with dangerous rocks, some of which are hidden just below the water's surface.

Men An Tol *Pencil 205 x 275 mm*

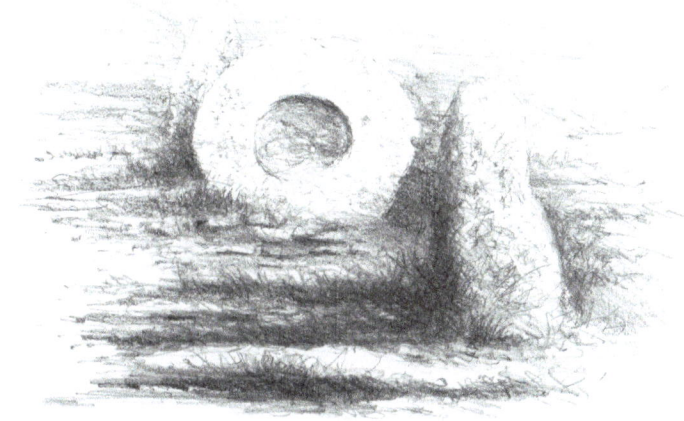

Some believe that these stones connect with fertility ceremonies. It is also said that they poses healing powers. Legendary mythology suggests that if someone crawls though the hole of the center rock then they will be cured of disease and illness.

Sea and Sky, West *Pencil 205 x 275 mm*

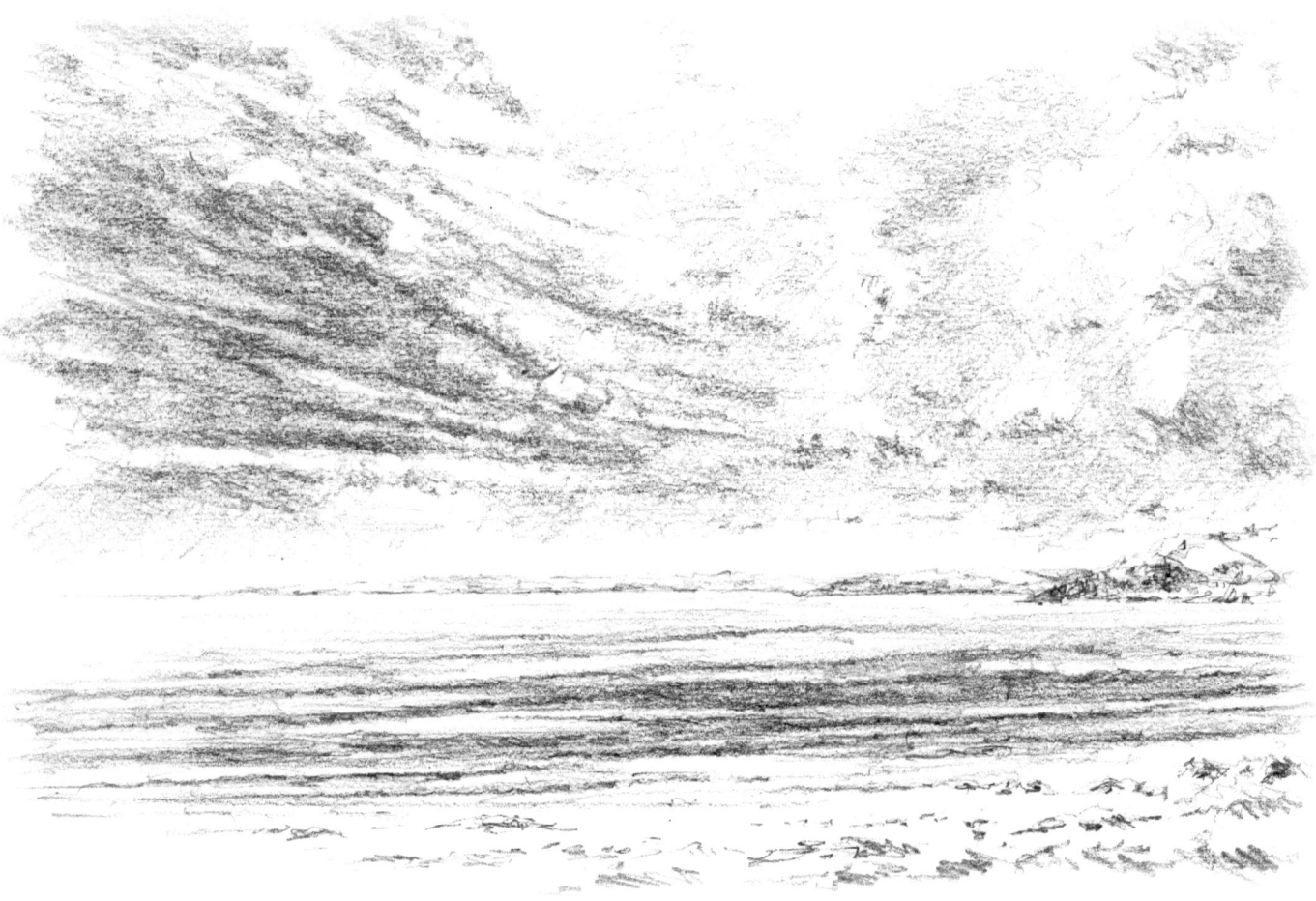

Rounding the western coastline is spectacular, the skies are an ever changing collider scope of form and colour. The sea and sky are natures perfect marriage. The water's surface is cloaked by high cliffs. Stunning as it maybe to the eye, many hundreds of shipwrecks have been claimed by this stretch of coast.

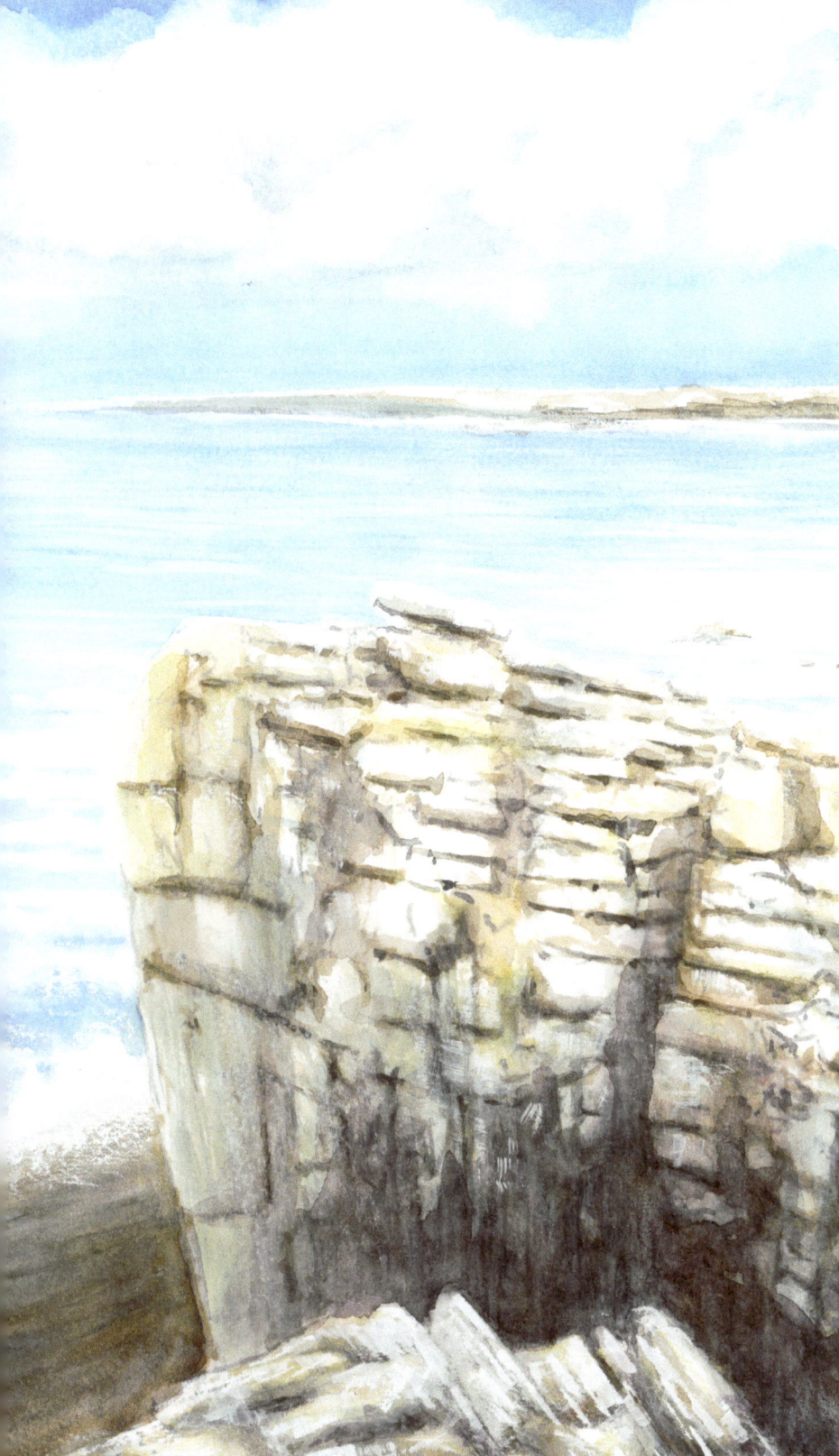

Sennen Cove
Watercolour 540 x 340 mm

My next stop off was at the marvelously beautiful Sennen Cove. This time I made a far more ambitious climb and painted the gigantic and seemingly precarious rock formations of that part of the coast.

Here the cliffs and rocks reach their upmost splendor. Far below these towering monuments the fury of the open sea performs a wild dance where high surf rolls towards the shoreline. Few places in the world offer more opportunities to the would be seascape artist than this place.

Lands End *Watercolour 340 x 540 mm*

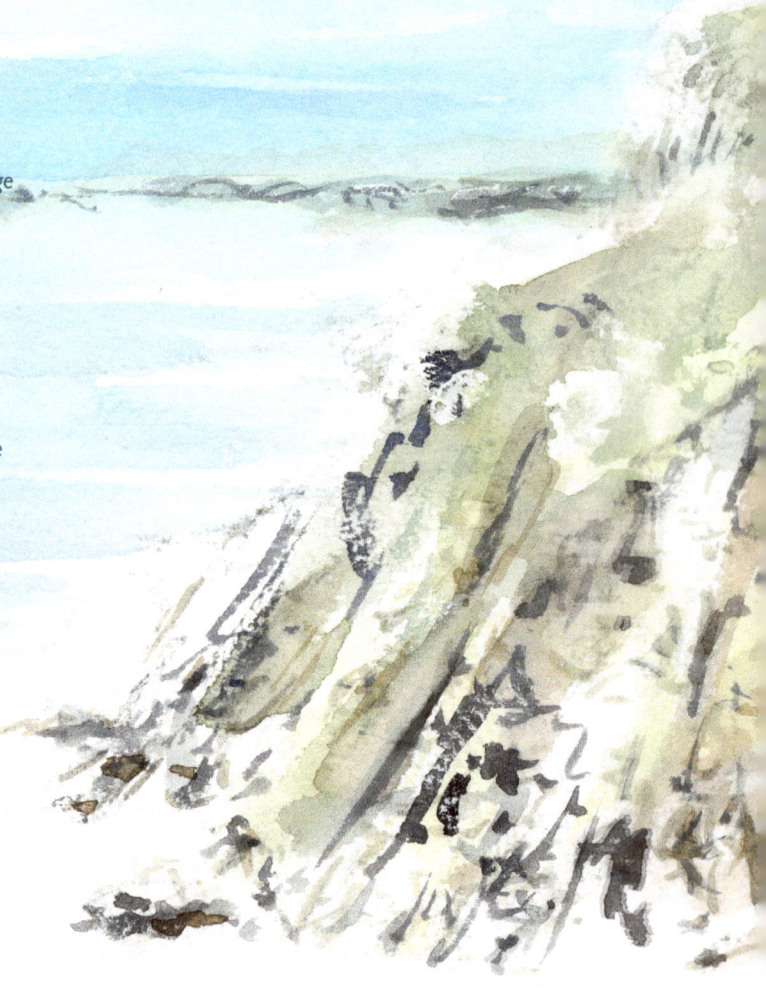

Just a few miles south sits Lands End. Many believe that it is there that is the most southerly point of the English coast, this is not true, it is in fact the most westerly point. What a coastline this is. At this south western edge of England the land meets the Celtic Sea and beyond that is the Atlantic Ocean, with nothing to hinder it's force as it is driven by tide and wind all the way from the shores of America. Here the drama of sea, land, and weather can be witnessed at it's most powerful.

The western tip of the Cornish Peninsula offers yet another spectacular vantage point to look out to the mighty Atlantic Ocean. The high cliffs are home to a myriad of birdlife, below these towering rock faces the current divides to feed of the Cornish North Shore and the English Channel. Here again is a most perfect place to paint, draw, or just reflect.

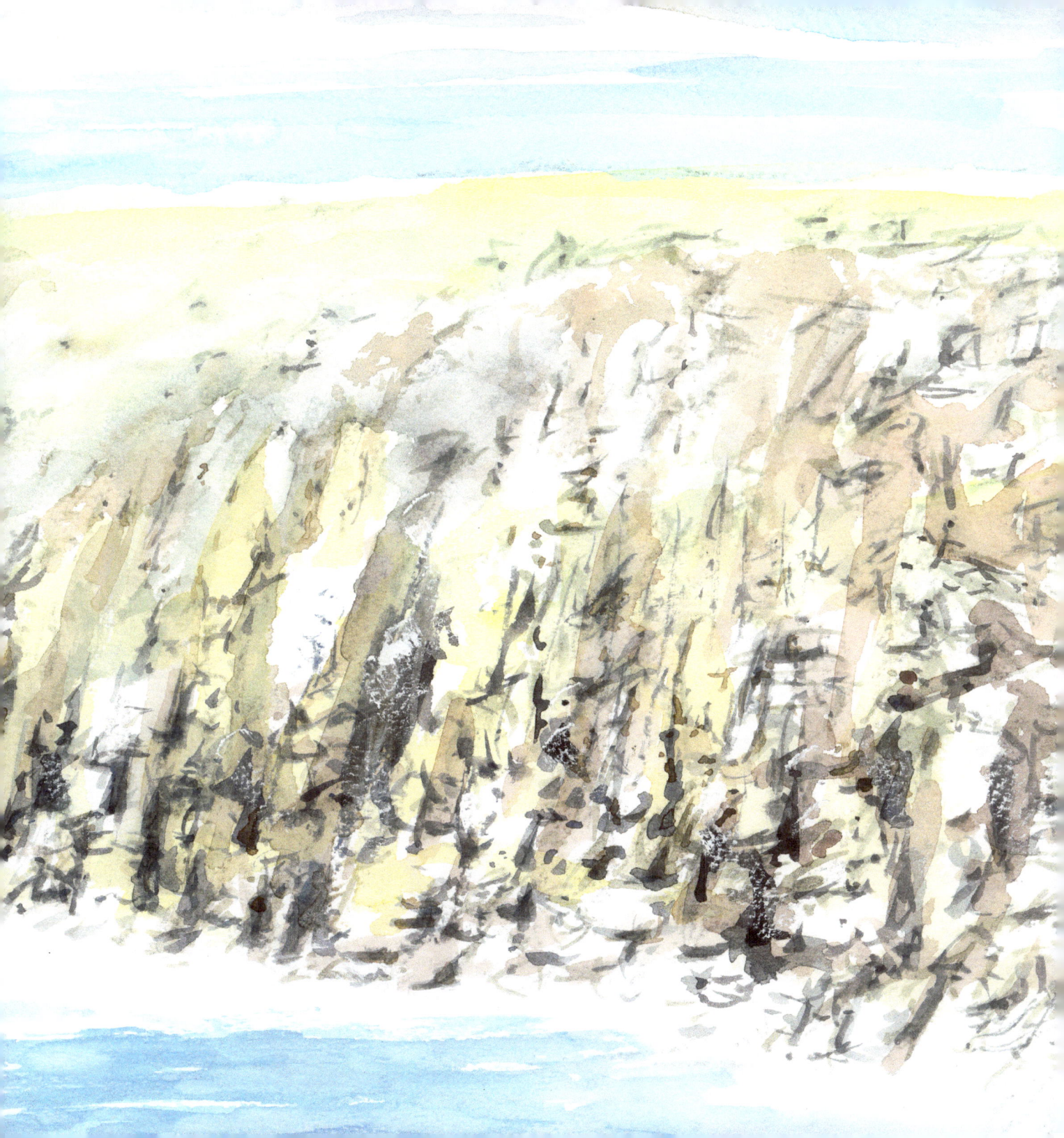

Gwennep Head

Watercolour 540 x 340 mm

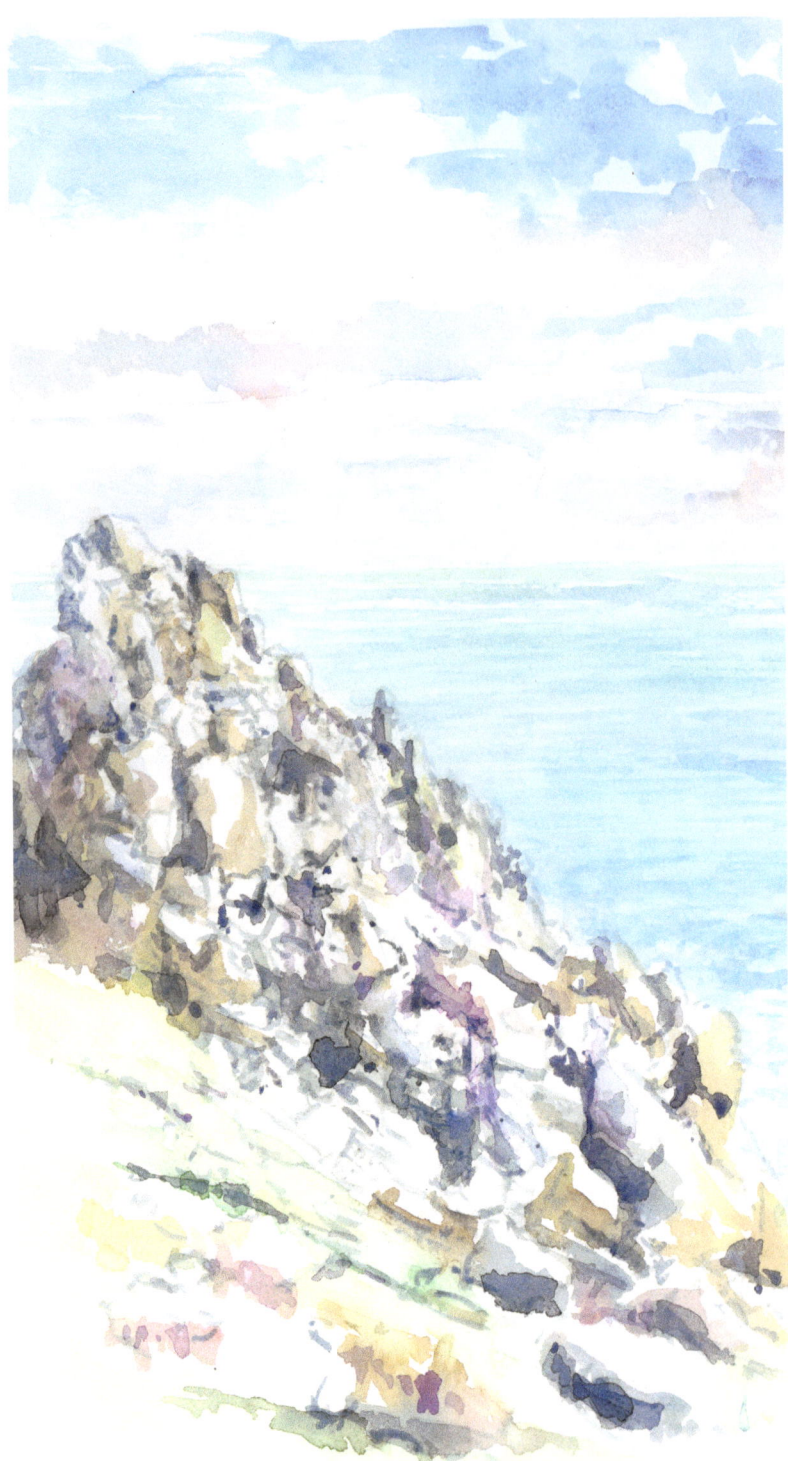

Next day, another hike and a climb. Some more guitar playing and painting. The location; Tol Pedn (its original Cornish name) better known as Gwenapp Head. The rocks there may well have been stacked by ancient giants, maybe in attempt to ensure that they would be remembered or even just for their amusement.

For the artist yet another impressive location to capture. It is not only the sea and rocks that make these seascapes so inspiring. They are complimented by the ever changing skies above. The visual scenario stimulates the senses; it is also the sounds and smells. In truth, I think it is near impossible to capture the moment with brush and pencil. I hope that my words and pictures encourage you to visit these places yourself.

Sunset *Watercolour 340 x 540 mm*

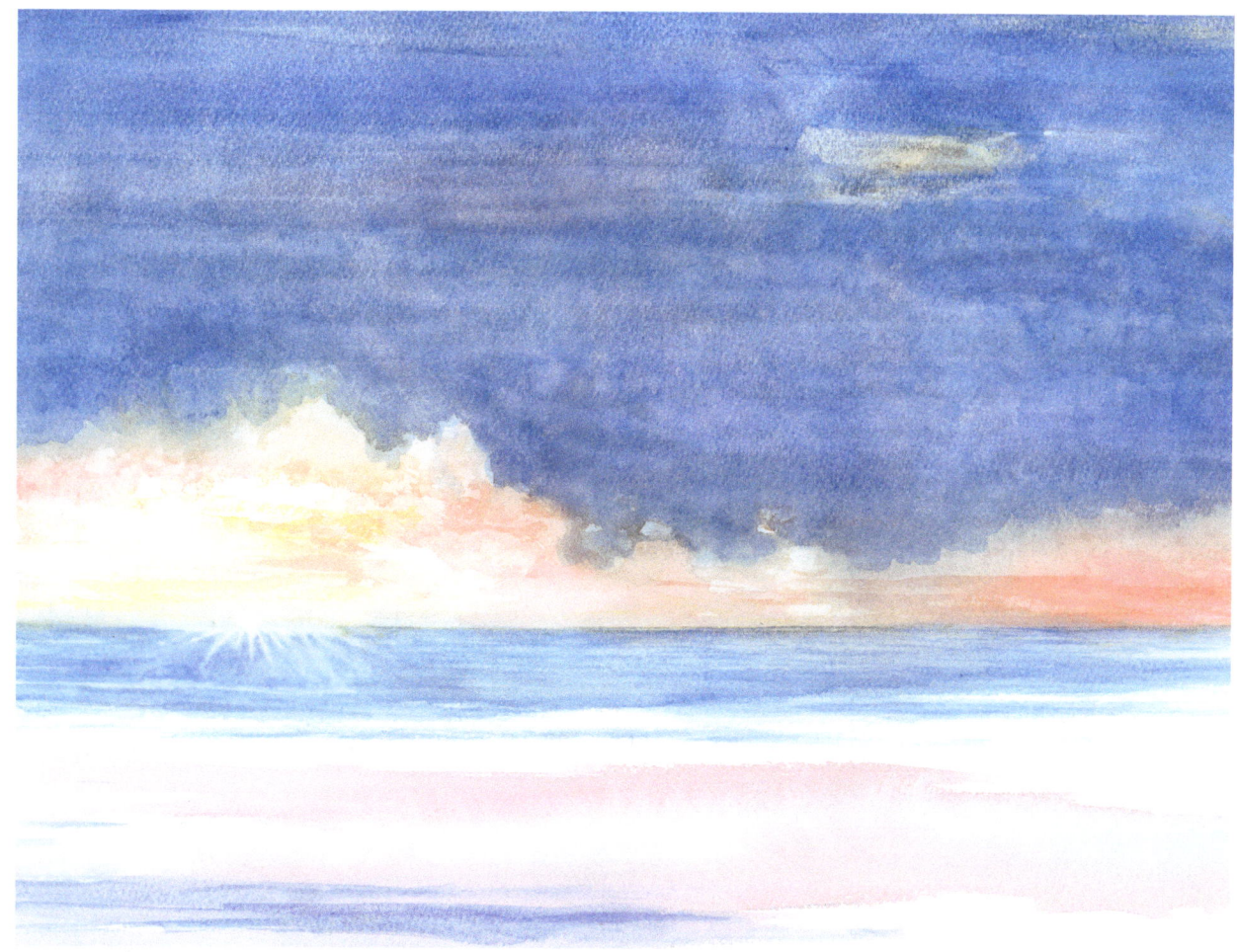

I continued around the truly most southerly headland of the UK, turned to the east and followed the trail along to my beloved Cape Cornwall. Along the way I made some pencil sketches of the breaking waves and painted a magnificent sunset.

Wild Cape Cornwall *Pencil 205 x 275 mm*

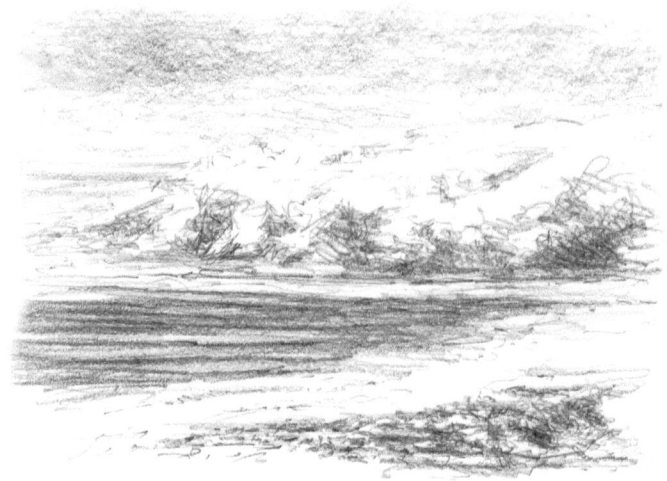

Sculpted by thousands of years of tide and weather the Cape is a magnificent place. The high cliff faces offer an ideal habitat to the wide variety of birdlife that occupies this coastline. Where the bottom of the cliffs meets the water the ocean has created deep caves that also host a multitude of marine life.

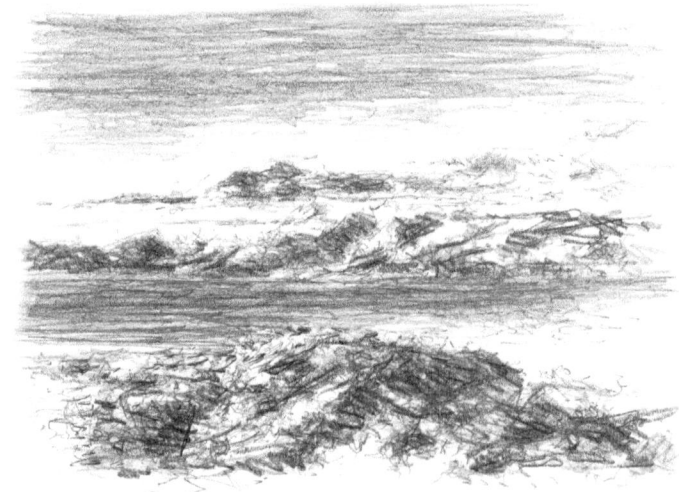

Rocks, Cape Cornwall *Pencil 205 x 275 mm*

The huge rocks that guard the shoreline defiantly remain immovable as the powerful waves break upon them. Raging as the sea often is here, it also can be so very calm. She remains always unpredictable and constantly changing.

Cape Cornwall's Raging Seas *Pencil 205 x 275 mm*

The drama of the high high waves that so often interact with this shoreline is a scenario that is heart moving. Sometimes the incoming tide is strengthened by an onshore wind. At other times the wind meets the tide head on causing giant plums of salt water to become airborne. Added to these factors of nature's concert is the strong current that edges this shoreline. An orchestration that is truly magnificent indeed.

Cat Rock *Watercolour 340 x 540 mm*

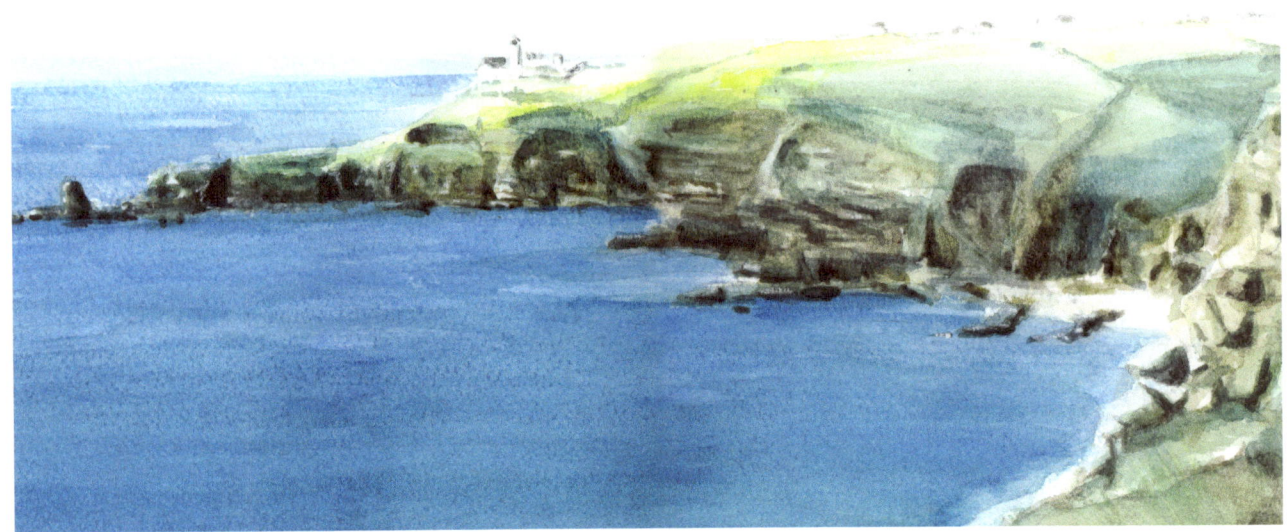

The next prominent geographical landmark is Lizard Point. To the east of the Lizard is Housel Bay. There the rocks protrude out into the bay and before they disappear beneath the water resides Cat Rock. This side of the Lizard the ocean is mostly of a calmer mood.

Reach For The Sky

Pencil 540 x 340 mm

I was at long last heading for my home in Falmouth but first I needed to round Rosemullion Point and to cross the Helford River. From St Anthony on the western bank I was forced to turn north again and as I made my way through the woods that line the Helford I sketched the high trees that seem to reach for the sky.

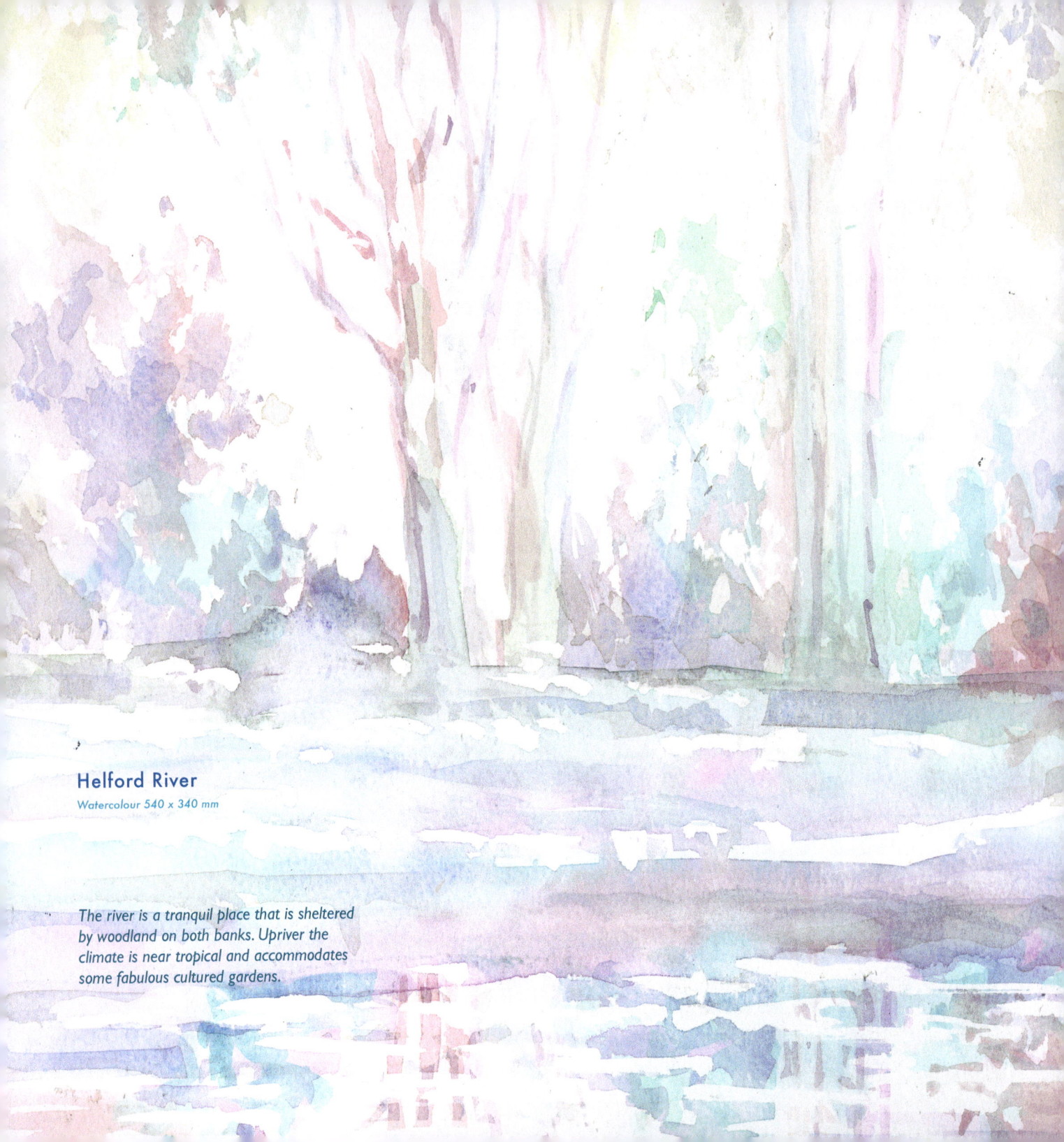

Helford River

Watercolour 540 x 340 mm

The river is a tranquil place that is sheltered by woodland on both banks. Upriver the climate is near tropical and accommodates some fabulous cultured gardens.

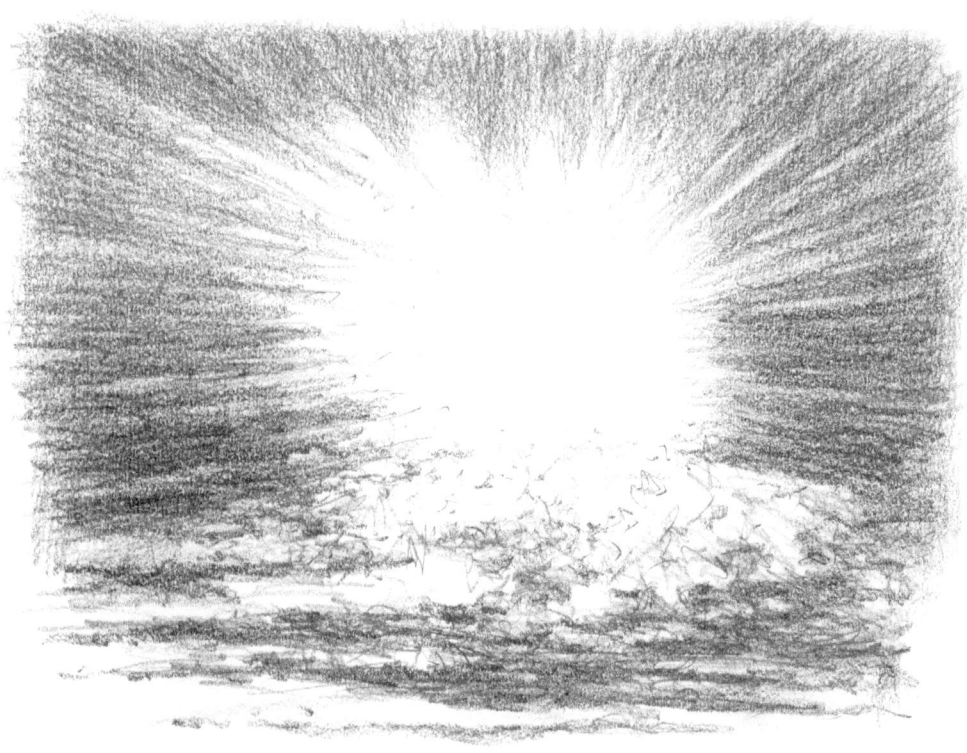

Sunburst
Pencil 250 x 250 mm

The best place to ever watch the sun come up is over the ocean.

Sound Of The Sea *Pencil 210 x 250 mm*

Following the coastal path that begins on the eastern side of the Helford River the ocean can be seen to offer up a tapestry of wave dances. Sometimes calm and quiet but on occasion she can rage.

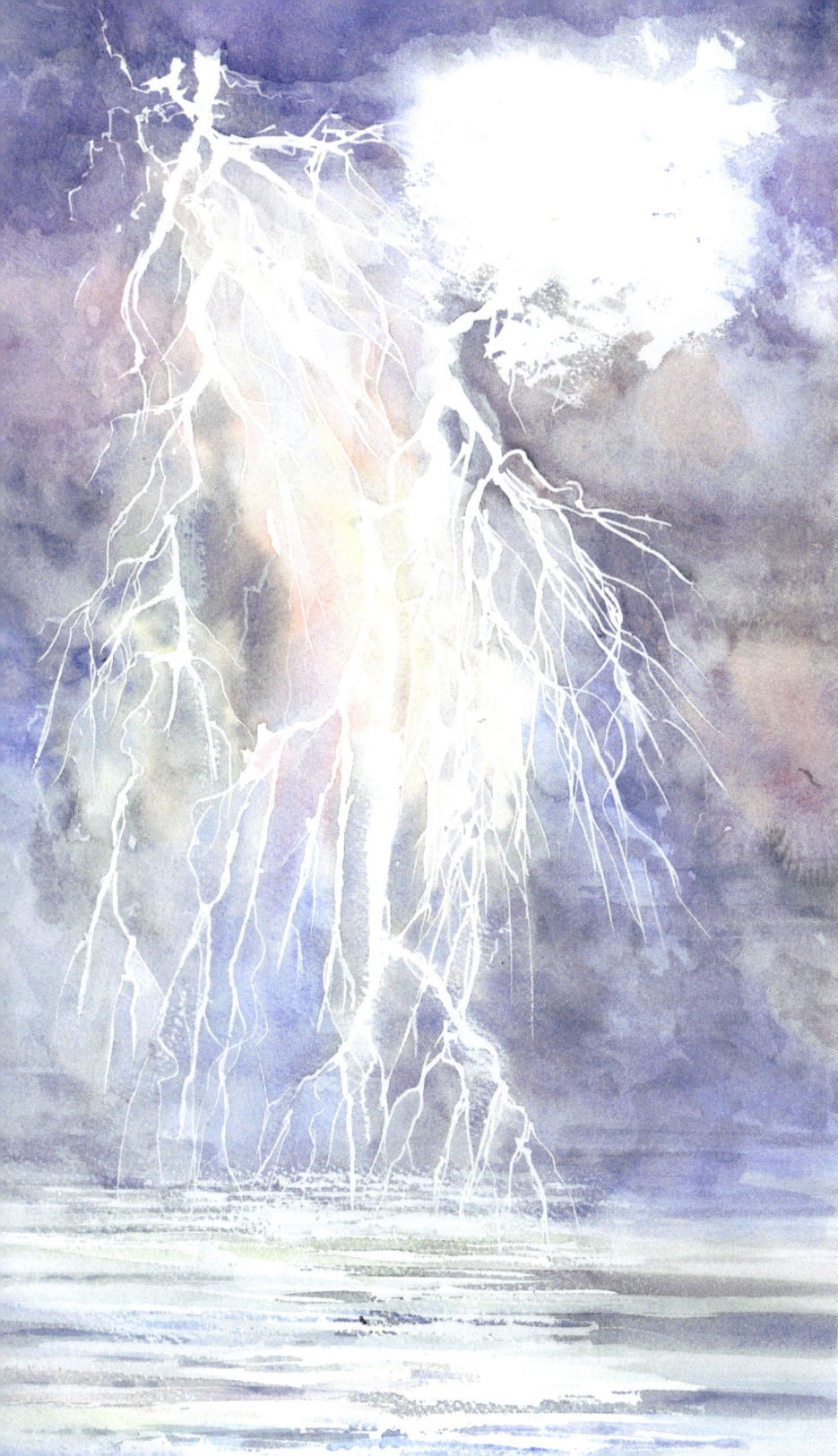

Thor

Watercolour 540 x 340 mm

The path leads onto Swanpool Beach and a storm breaks. The sound of thunder becomes deafening and bolts of lighting illuminate the sky. The drama is reflected on the oceans surface as far out as the eye can see.

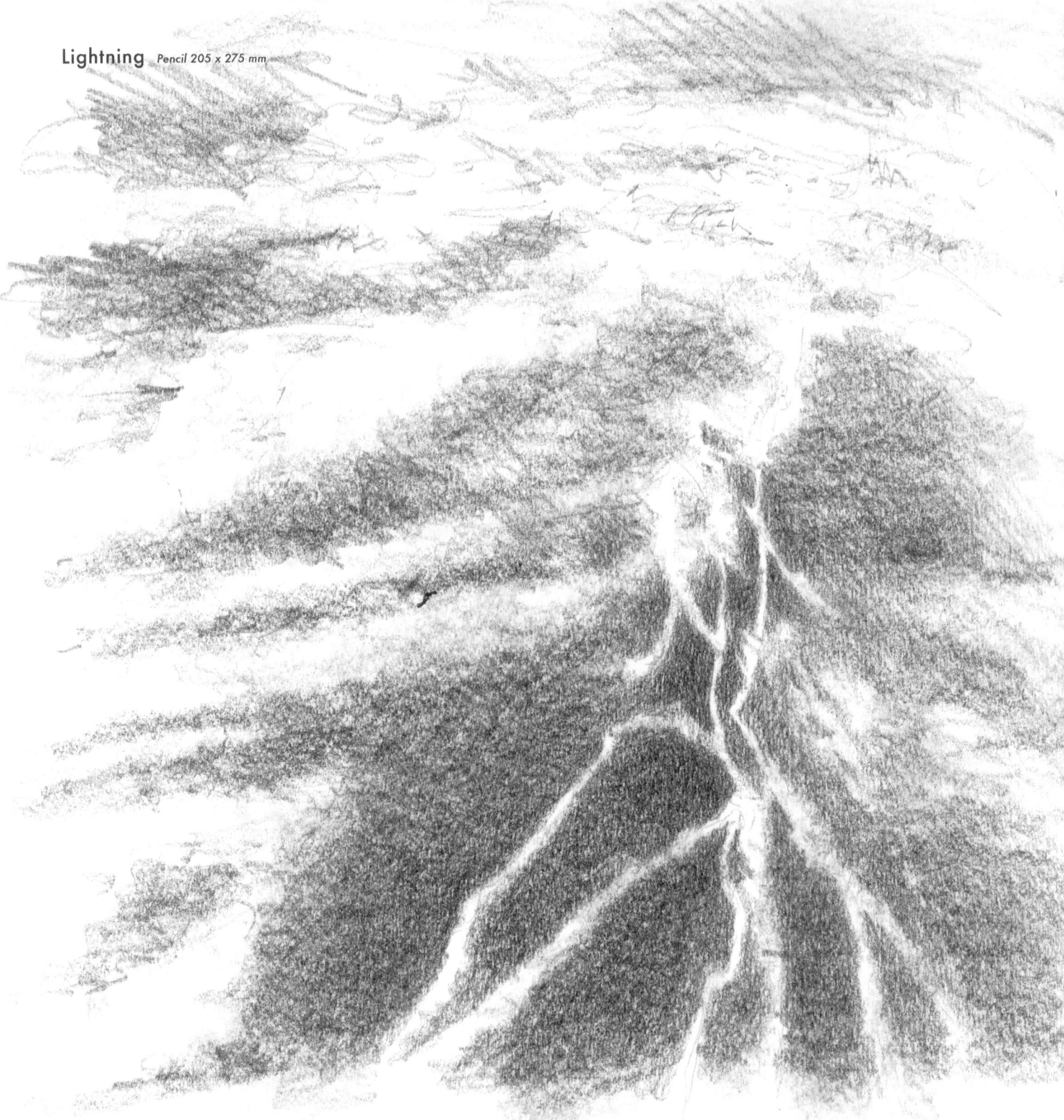

Lightning *Pencil 205 x 275 mm*

The Gateway Watercolour 340 x 540 mm

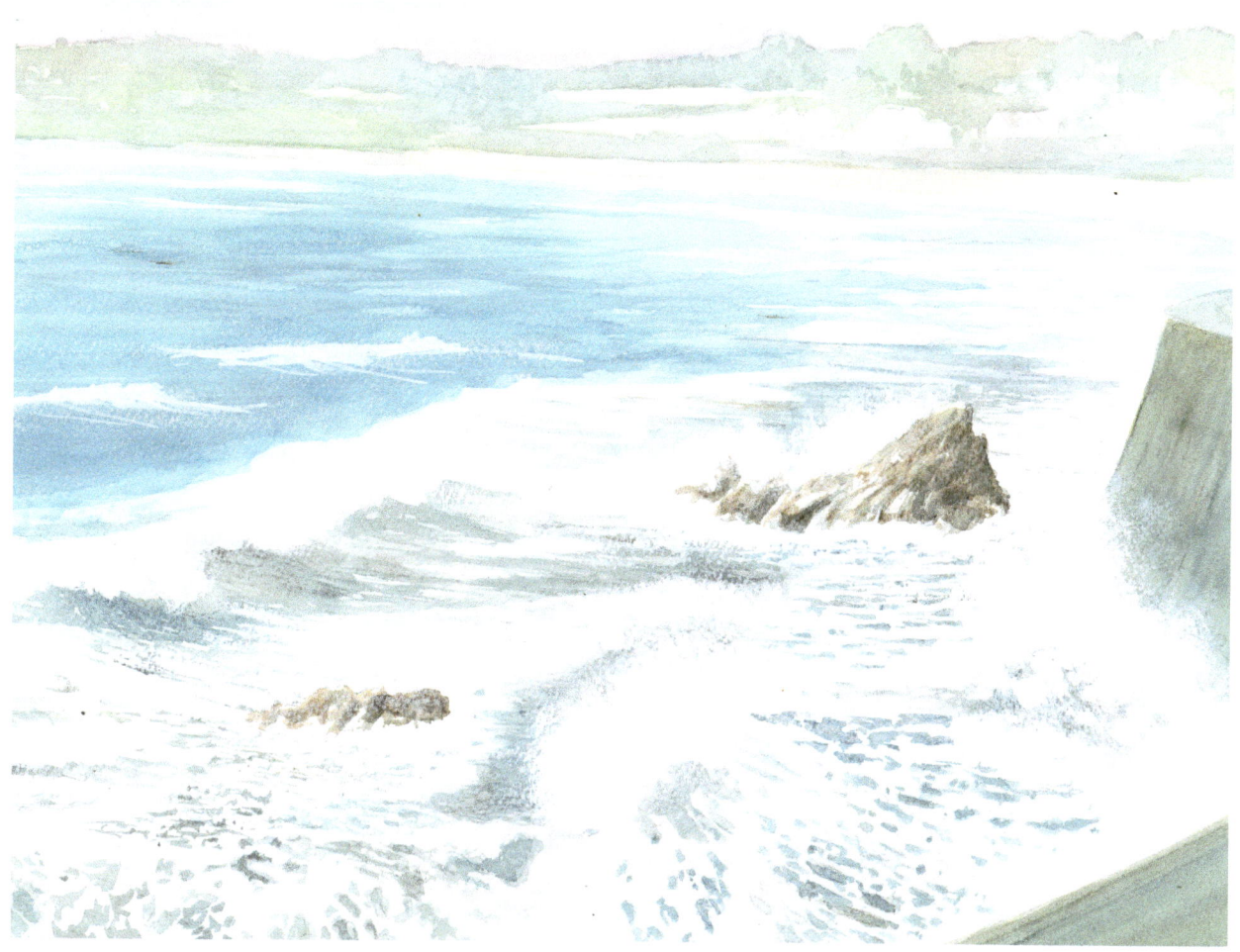

So many times I've walked this wall. Countless sea states and weather conditions I have encountered here. The only thing that is not under constant change is the rock that marks where the wall curves in towards the beach. The narrow gap between the rock and the wall always puts me in mind of a gateway leading to one of my most favourite locations.

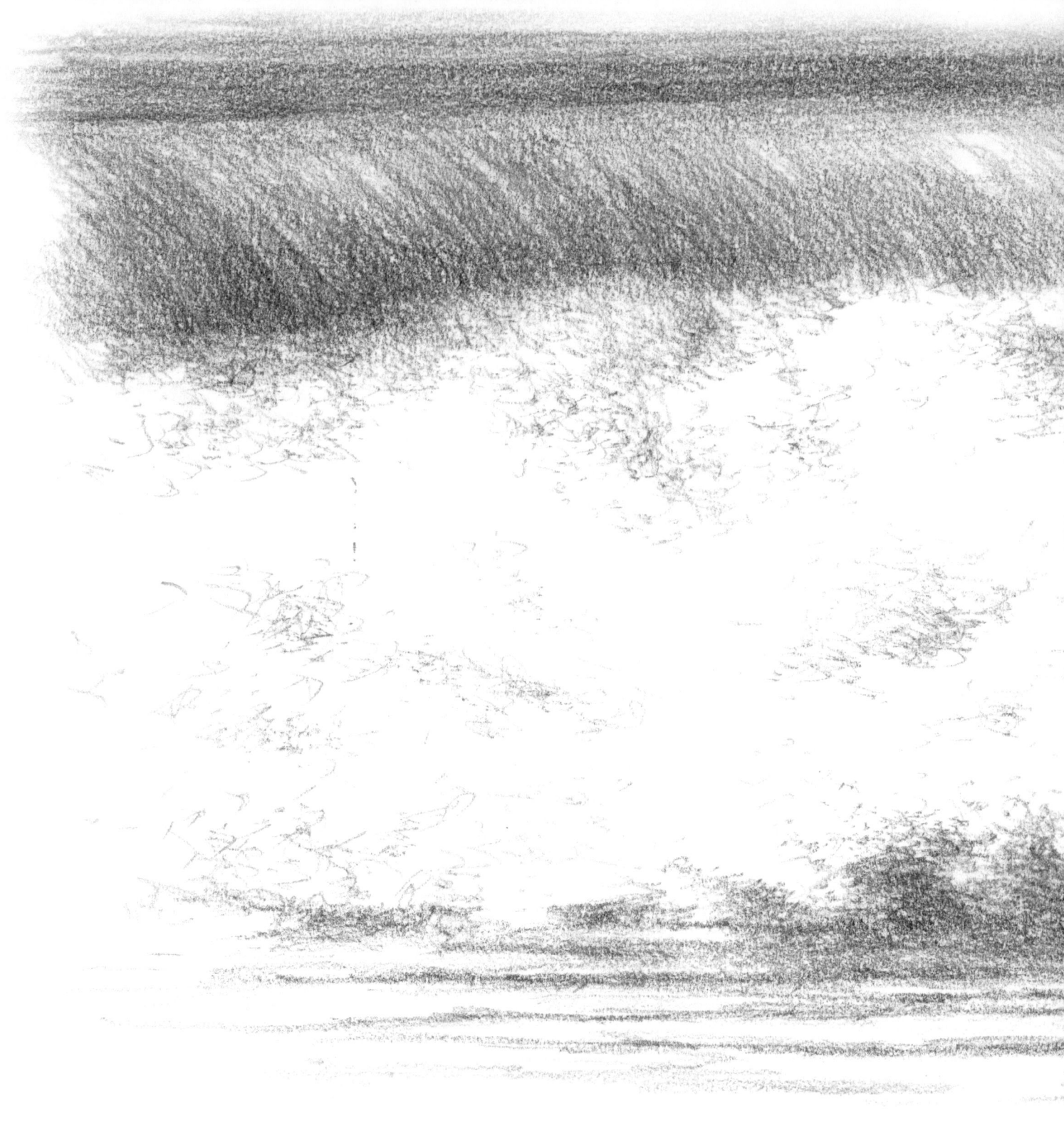

Breaking Roller
Pencil 340 x 540 mm

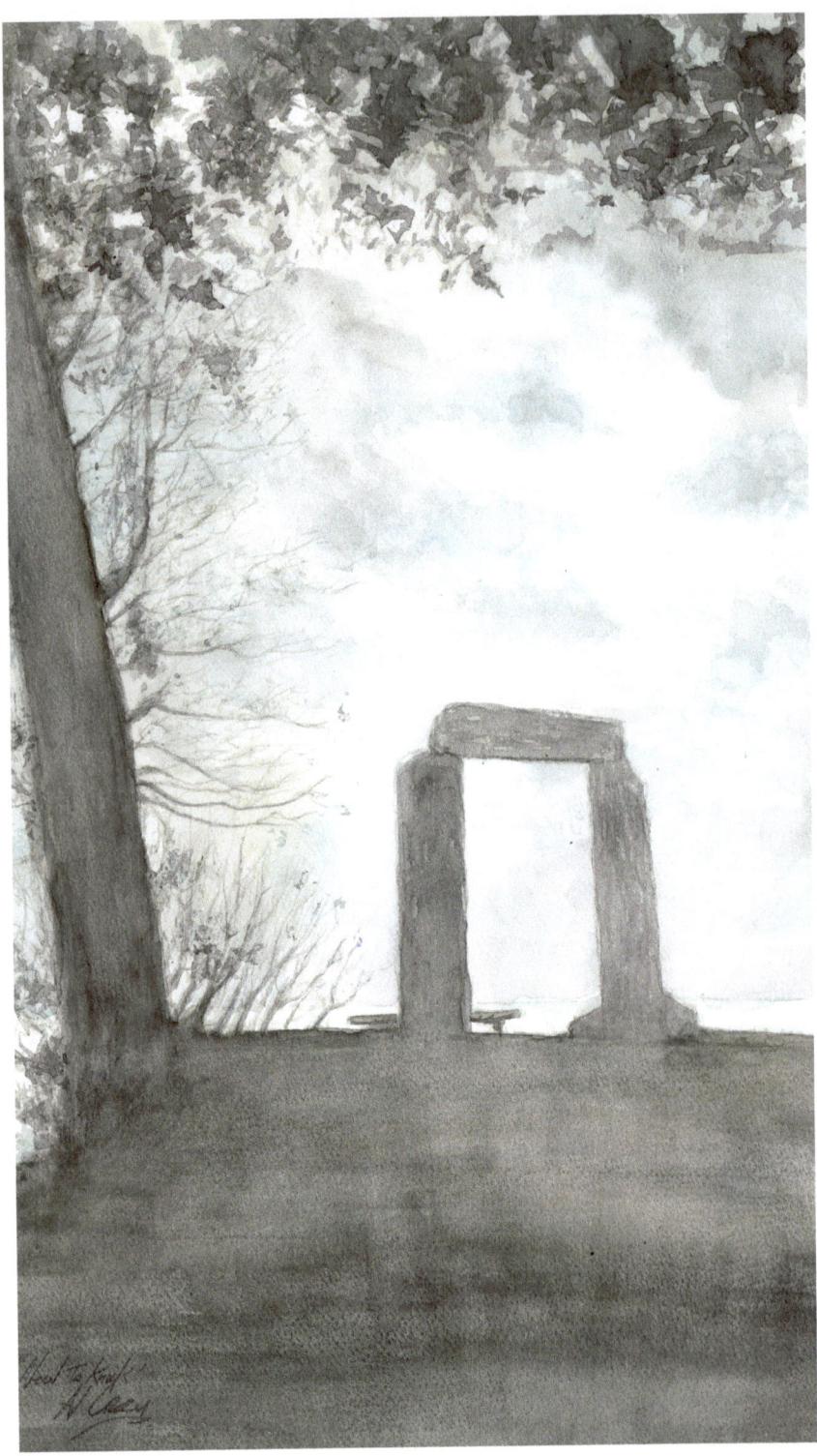

No Need To Knock
Watercolour 540 x 340 mm

Beneath this huge stone archway is a bench where one can gaze out to sea and let the mind wonder. It is a welcoming spot where in summer the sent of flowers and the salt air fills the senses. Or on a stormy night it is an ideal place to watch lightning fill the sky.

Falmouth Docks
Watercolour 340 x 540 mm

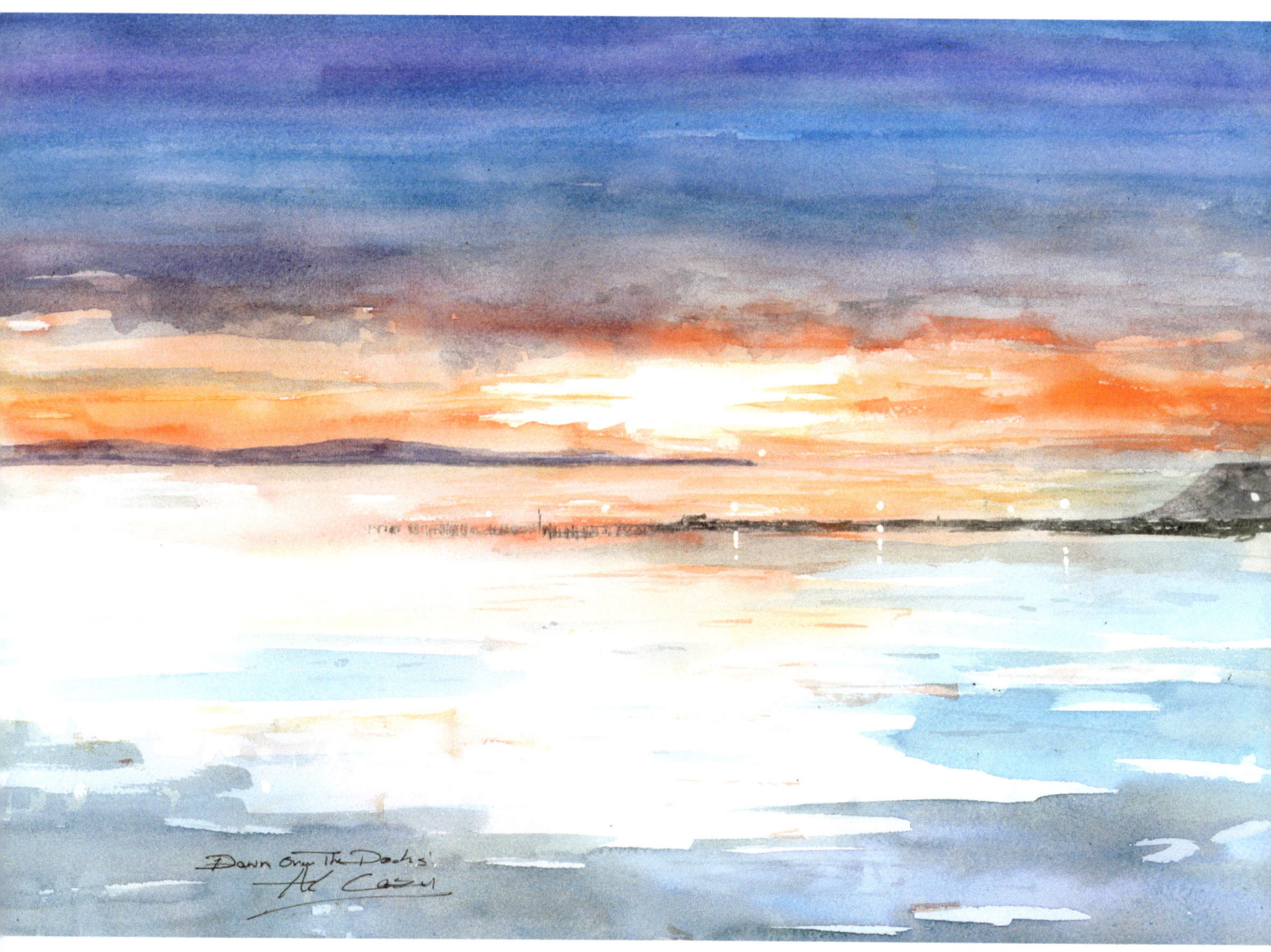

Dawn over the Docks

Falmouth boasts to be the third largest natural deep water port in the world. It is also the first adequate port for very large ships entering the English Channel. It hosts commercial vessels, luxury cruisers, and domestic craft. The shipyard here is very large and contracts to repair and refit very big commercial ships and ferries as well as the designing and building of luxury yachts. Although these docks are a hive of busy activity, at times they can be a tranquil place, as can be seen in this beautiful sunrise over the docks.

Pendennis Castle Pencil 205 x 275 mm

Above the high headland that overlooks the
mouth of the Fal River is Pendennis Castle.
Commissioned by king Henry the Eightieth
it was originally intended to protect Cornwall
and England against a Spanish invasion.

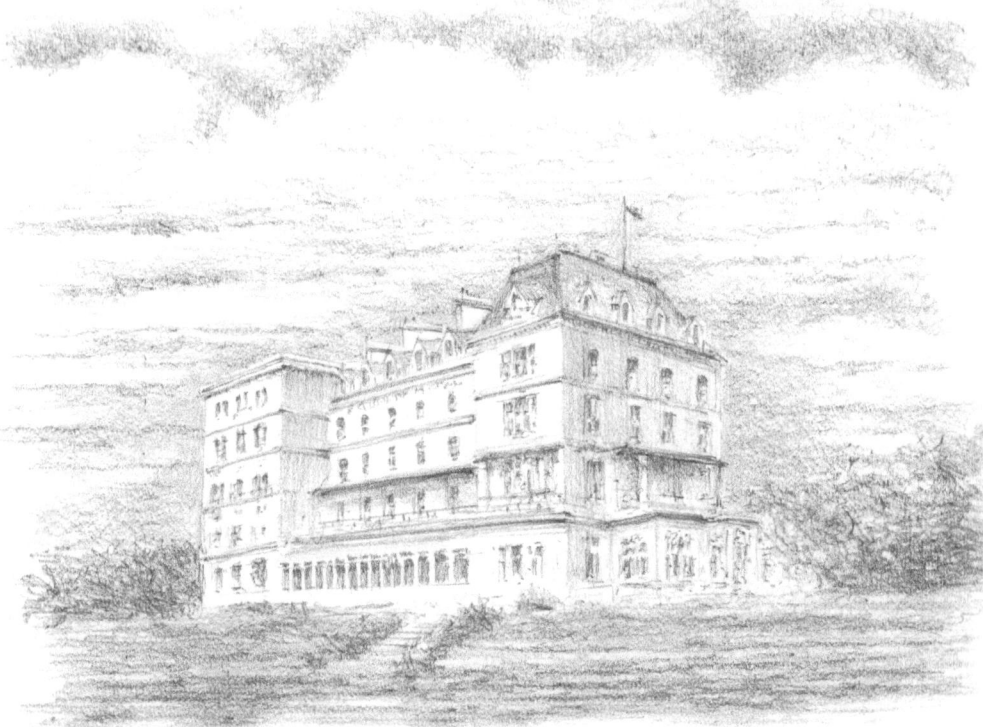

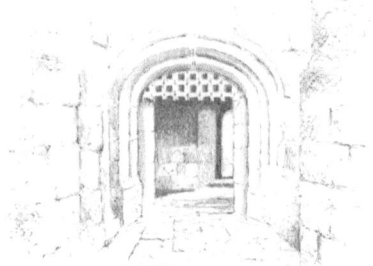

Falmouth Hotel Pencil 205 x 275 mm

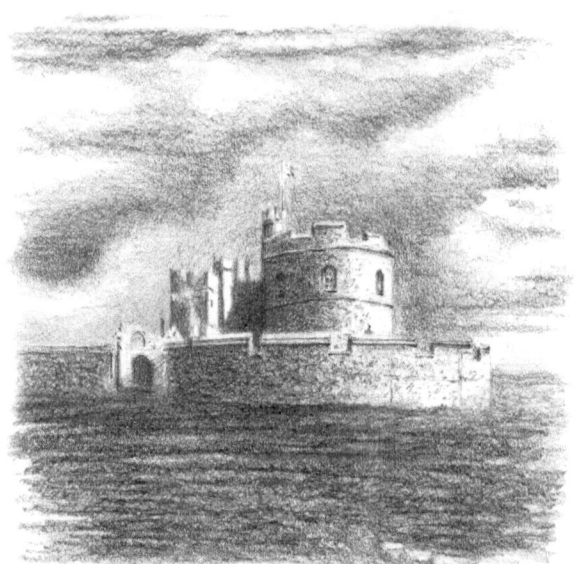

I'm home! This is where I have now
lived for more than ten years. It
overlooks Castle Beach, from there the
seawall provides a route to Tunnel Beach,
a private place that is good for playing
music, swimming, writing, and
making pictures.

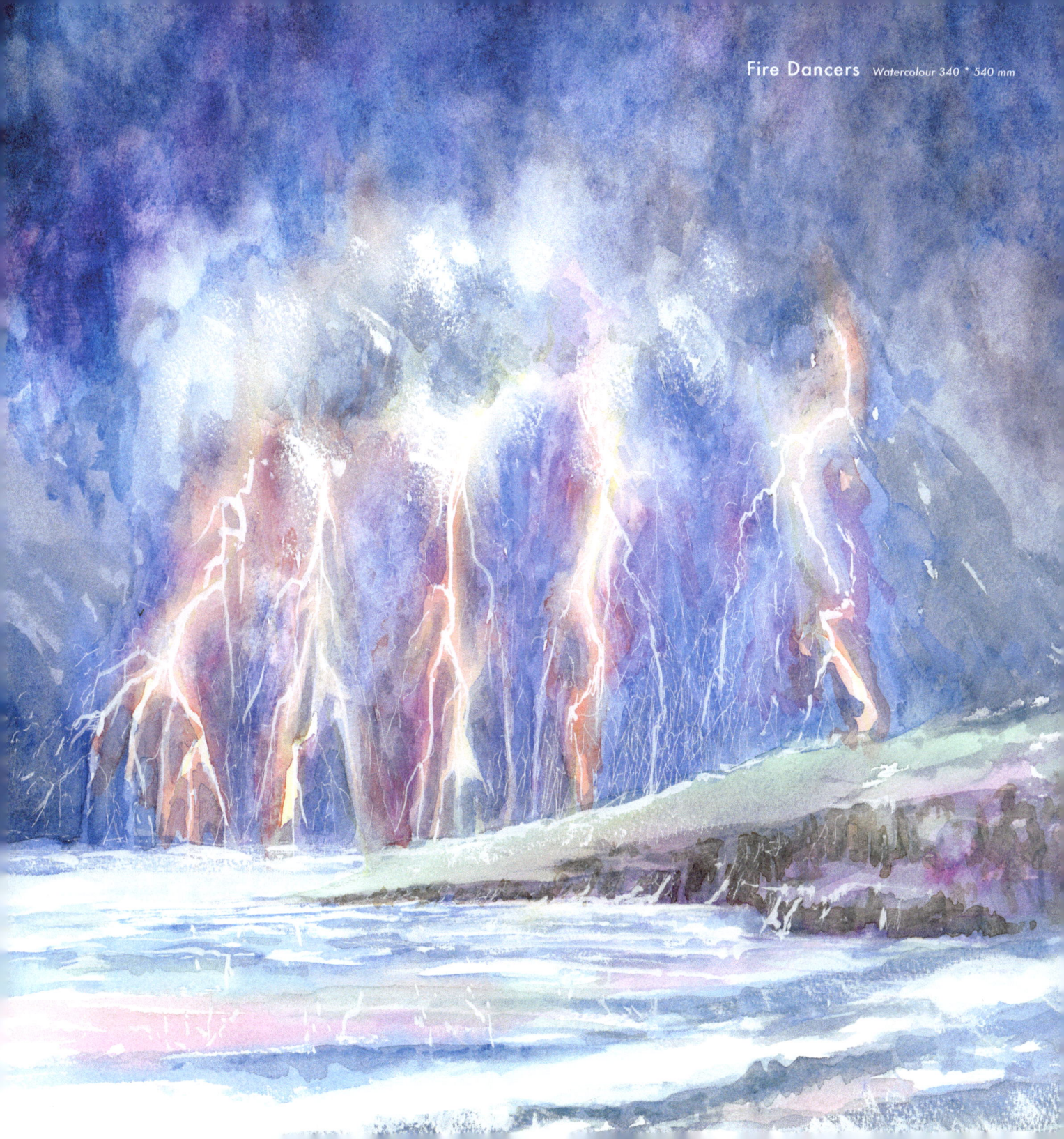

Fire Dancers Watercolour 340 * 540 mm

Crescent Moon Over The Castle

Pencil 340 x 540 mm

So many times I've watched the sun go down and the moon appear over this magical headland. If ghosts do exist then I'm sure that they abide in this place. Maybe some of them once inhabited this ancient castle that overlooks the entrance to the river.

Little Egypt *Watercolour 340 x 540 mm*

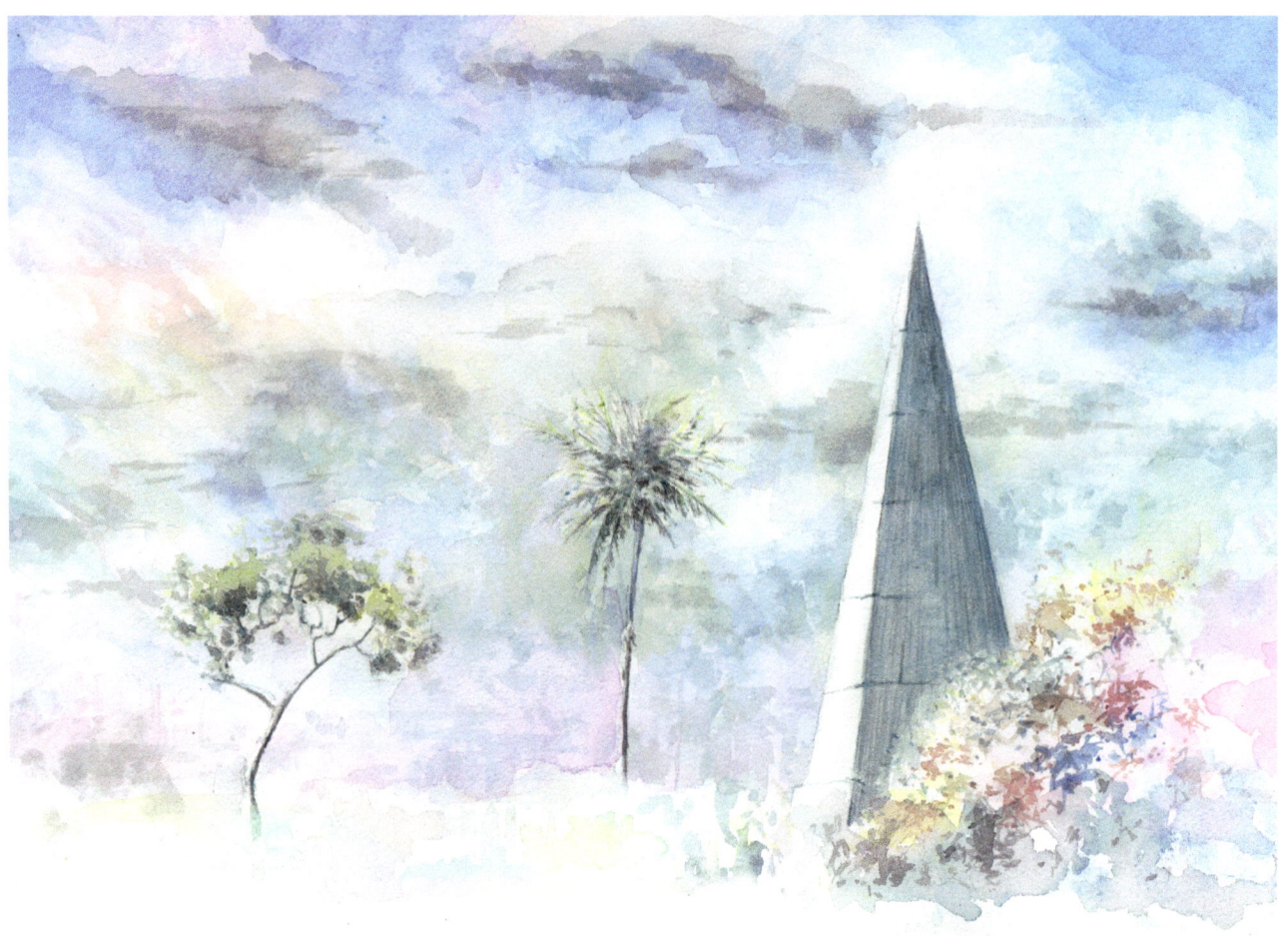

Falmouth Town, the memorial stone aside the tree with copper coloured leaves and the tall palms reminds me of some Egyptian scene that may have been painted during the eighteen hundreds. I'm home and the map is complete. It's a matter of how you see things and from where. Remember the riddle?

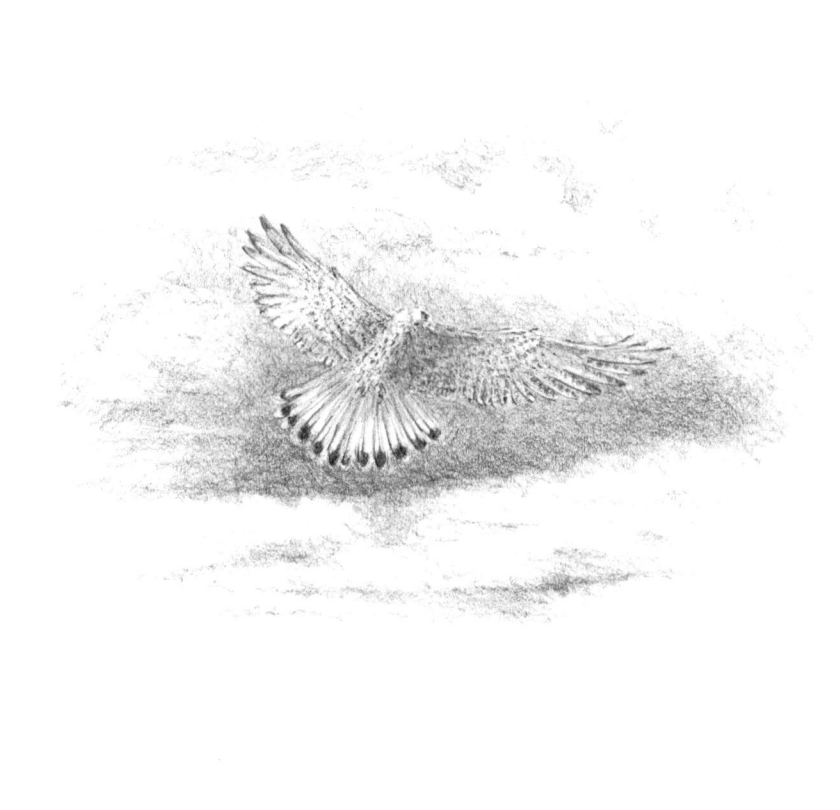

CORNWALL
Coast to Coast

Artwork by Al Cazu (Alan G Williamson)

Cazu

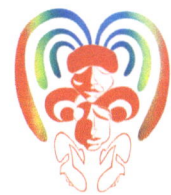

Productions & Publishing

e-mail: mail@alcazu.com

Tel: 07745606275

To view a full catalogue of artwork
by Al Cazu:
www.cazu.co.uk

www.ingramcontent.com/pod-product-compliance
Lightning Source LLC
Chambersburg PA
CBHW050818180526
45159CB00004B/1708

9 781523 885237